CRIME VICTIMS' RIGHTS ACT

Crime Victims' Rights Act

Charles Doyle

Novinka Books
New York

For permission to use material from this book please contact us:
Telephone 631-231-7269; Fax 631-231-8175
Web Site: http://www.novapublishers.com

LIBRARY OF CONGRESS CATALOGING-IN-PUBLICATION DATA

Doyle, Charles.

Crime Victims' Rights Act / Charles Doyle.

p. cm.

ISBN 978-1-60456-525-6 (softcover)

1. Victims of crimes--Legal status, laws, etc.--United States. 2. Reparation (Criminal justice)--United States. 3. Victims of crimes--Legal status, laws, etc.--United States--Cases. 4. Reparation (Criminal justice)--United States--Cases. I. Title. KF9763.D69 2008 344.7303'288--dc22

2008012917

Published by Nova Science Publishers, Inc. New York

CONTENTS

PREFACE

Legal reform in the name of victims of crime began to appear in state and federal law in the 1960's. It can be seen in victim restitution and compensation laws, in the reform of rape laws, drunk driving statutes, bail laws, and in provisions for victim impact statements at sentencing, to name a few. Over time in many jurisdictions these specific victim provisions were joined by a more general, more comprehensive victims' bills of rights. Thus, by the close of the twentieth century, thirty-three states had added victims' rights amendments to their state constitutions and each of the states had general statutory declarations of victims' rights.

Chapter 1

CRIME VICTIMS' RIGHTS ACT: A SUMMARY AND LEGAL ANALYSIS OF 18 U.S.C. 3771*

SUMMARY

Section 3771 of title 18 of the United States Code is a statutory bill of rights for victims of crimes committed in violation of federal law or the laws of the District of Columbia. It defines victims as anyone directly and proximately harmed by such an offense, individuals and legal entities alike. It does not appear to include family relatives of a deceased, child or incapacitated victim except in a representative capacity.

Numbered among the rights it conveys are (1) the right to be reasonably protected from the accused, (2) the right to notification of public court and parole proceedings and of any release of the accused, (3) the right not to be excluded from public court proceedings under most circumstances, (4) the right to be heard in public court proceedings relating to bail, the acceptance of a plea bargain, sentencing, or parole, (5) the right to confer with the prosecutor, (6) the right to restitution under the law, (7) the right to proceedings free from unwarranted delays, and (8) the right to be treated fairly and with respect to one's dignity and privacy.

* Excerpted from CRS Report RL33679, Updated September 29, 2006

The section directs the courts and law enforcement officials to see to it that the rights it creates are honored. Both victims and prosecutors may assert the rights and seek review from the appellate courts should the rights be initially denied.

The section vests no rights in the accused nor does it create cause of action damages in any instance where a victim is afforded less than the section's full benefits.

The Justice Department regulations that the section calls for must include the designation of an official to receive victim complaints concerning performance under the section, training for Justice Department employees, and disciplinary sanctions for willful and wanton violations. The text of the section is appended.

INTRODUCTION

The victims of federal crimes enjoy certain rights to notice, attendance and participation in the federal criminal justice process by virtue of 18 U.S.C. 3771.[1] More specifically, the section assures victims that they have:

(1) The right to be reasonably protected from the accused.
(2) The right to reasonable, accurate, and timely notice of any public court proceeding, or any parole proceeding, involving the crime or of any release or escape of the accused.
(3) The right not to be excluded from any such public court proceeding, unless the court, after receiving clear and convincing evidence, determines that testimony by the victim would be materially altered if the victim heard other testimony at that proceeding.
(4) The right to be reasonably heard at any public proceeding in the district court involving release, plea, sentencing, or any parole proceeding.
(5) The reasonable right to confer with the attorney for the Government in the case.
(6) The right to full and timely restitution as provided in law.
(7) The right to proceedings free from unreasonable delay.
(8) The right to be treated with fairness and with respect for the victim's dignity and privacy. 18 U.S.C. 3771(a).

Section 3771 is the product of a long effort to afford greater deference to victims in the criminal justice process. It is akin to the victims' bill of rights provisions found in the laws of the various states and augments a fairly wide variety of pre-existing federal victims' rights legislation. Its enactment followed closely on the heels of discontinued efforts to pass a victims' rights amendment to the United States Constitution.

BACKGROUND

Legal reform in the name of victims of crime began to appear in state and federal law in the 1960's. It can be seen in victim restitution and compensation laws,[2] in the reform of rape laws,[3] drunk driving statutes,[4] bail laws,[5] and in provisions for victim impact statements at sentencing,[6] to name a few. Over time in many jurisdictions these specific victim provisions were joined by a more general, more comprehensive victims' bills of rights. Thus, by the close of the twentieth century, thirty-three states had added a victims' rights amendments to their state constitutions[7] and each of the states had general statutory declaration of victims' rights.[8]

In the meantime, Congress had enacted a series of individual victims' rights provisions[9] as well as a general aspirational federal statute directed to the performance of federal officials:

Victims' Rights

(a) *Best efforts to accord rights.* Officers and employees of the Department of Justice and other departments and agencies of the United States engaged in the detection, investigation, or prosecution of crime shall make their best efforts to see that victims of crime are accorded the rights described in subsection (b) of this section.

(b) *Rights of crime victims.* A crime victim has the following rights:

(1) The right to be treated with fairness and with respect for the victim's dignity and privacy.
(2) The right to be reasonably protected from the accused offender.
(3) The right to be notified of court proceedings.
(4) The right to be present at all public court proceedings related to the offense, unless the court determines that testimony by the

victim would be materially affected if the victim heard other testimony at trial.

(5) The right to confer with [the] attorney for the Government in the case.

(6) The right to restitution.

(7) The right to information about the conviction, sentencing, imprisonment, and release of the offender.

(c) *No cause of action or defense.* This section does not create a cause of action or defense in favor of any person arising out of the failure to accord to a victim the rights enumerated in subsection (b) of this section. 104 Stat. 4820, 42 U.S.C. 10606 (2000 ed.).[10]

Section 10606 was accompanied by a statement of the sense of Congress encouraging similar action by the states[11] and by specific directions to the heads of the various federal law enforcement departments and agencies for implementation.[12]

Moreover beginning in the 104th Congress, both Houses regularly considered victims' rights amendments to the United States Constitution.[13] Unable to reach the consensus necessary for passage, sponsors opted for a statutory substitute,[14] which unlike the "best-efforts" preexisting statute, included enforcement mechanisms. The legislation, S. 2329 — the Scott Campbell, Stephanie Roper, Wendy Preston, Louarna Gillis, and Nila Lynn Crime Victims' Right Act — was introduced in Senate on April 21, 2004 and passed the following day.[15] The House merged an amended version of S. 2329 with DNA proposals in H.R. 5107, the Justice for All Act, which it passed on October 6, 2004.[16] The Senate passed the H.R. 5107 unamended three days later,[17] and the President signed it on October 30, 2004.[18]

WHO IS A VICTIM?

The definition of "victim," the question of deciding who should be afforded rights and who should not be, was one of the difficulties that surfaced during the course of debates over the proposals to amend the United States Constitution. Sponsors of the 108th Congress proposals had opted not to include a specific definition of victim, but had referred to the rights as those of the "victims of *violent* crimes," S.J.Res.1/ H.J.Res. 48 (108th Cong.). In doing so, they excluded the victims of fraud, regardless of how extensive or devastating the crime, a result some would consider unsatisfactory.[19]

Section 3771 suffers no such limitation and thus would appear to be available to victims of both violent and nonviolent crimes.[20]

Section 3771 also provides an explicit definition:

> For the purposes of this chapter, the term "crime victim" means a person directly and proximately harmed as a result of the commission of a Federal offense or an offense in the District of Columbia. In the case of a crime victim who is under 18 years of age, incompetent, incapacitated, or deceased, the legal guardians of the crime victim or the representatives of the crime victim's estate, family members, or any other persons appointed as suitable by the court, may assume the crime victim's rights under this chapter, but in no event shall the defendant be named as such guardian or representative. 18 U.S.C. 3771(e).

Other than the coverage of victims of crime under the laws of the District of Columbia, the definition is by and large the same definition found in the general federal restitution statutes, 18 U.S.C. 3663, 3663A. Commentators have suggested that courts will be able to draw upon the case law developed under the two restitution statutes to determine who qualifies as a victim under section 3771.[21] Recourse may be somewhat complicated, however, by the presence of additional language in the restitution definitions,[22] or by the references in the restitution statutes to specific persons[23] and the types of harm that qualify for restitution.[24]

Restitution Case Law: Entities

Nevertheless, the courts do seem likely to consult their experience under the restitution statutes when construing section 3771's definition of victim. Section 3771 and the restitution statutes speak of victims who are "persons" ("'crime victim' means a person . . ."). Although in common parlance, this might be thought to restrict the class of victims to human beings, general usage within the United States Code is to the contrary. Unless the context suggests another intent, the word "person" as used in the United States Code is understood to "include corporations, companies, associations, firms, partnerships, societies, and joint stock companies as well as individuals," 1 U.S.C. 1.

Earlier cases rejected arguments that only human beings could be "victims" qualified for restitution.[25] Perhaps because the question is considered settled, the argument has disappeared, and later courts have regularly found restitution appropriate for legal entities without commenting upon their want of human status.[26] The universal definition in 1 U.S.C. 1 does not mention governmental entities, but they too have been found qualified for restitution under the appropriate circumstances.[27]

Restitution Case Law: Directly and Proximately Harmed

An earlier version of the restitution statutes authorized restitution for injuries and losses resulting from certain offenses but made no mention of direct and proximate harm, 18 U.S.C. 3579, 3580 (1982 ed.). "This [earlier] language suggest[ed] persuasively that Congress intended restitution to be tied to the loss caused by the offense of conviction," the Supreme Court said in *Hughey v. United States*, 495 U.S. 411, 418 (1990). Thus, a restitution order might be based only upon the offenses to which the defendant had plead and not upon the additional offenses for which he had been initially indicted, *Id.* at 422. After the restitution statutes were rewritten to include the "direct and proximate" language, some courts have continued to hold to the proposition that restitution is only available for harm directly related to the crime of conviction or provided for in some explicit exception such as that available for conspiracies and plea bargains.[28] Other courts have permitted restitution based on proximate harm if it is not too remote from the crime of conviction and if there are no unrelated intervening causes or contributors to the harm.[29] Thus for instance, a defendant convicted of bank robbery may be order to pay restitution for the damage he caused during his attempted getaway.[30]

Restitution Case Law: Crime of Conviction

Under sections 3663 and 3663A restitution is only available for harm related to the crime of conviction. Victims of crimes, other than those for which the defendant is convicted, are not entitled to restitution even if they were victims of offenses that were initially charged with the crime of conviction or are undisputably related to the crime of conviction.[31]

The same may hold true for victims under section 3771. Individuals may lose victim status under section 3771 during the course the criminal proceedings if charges covering the crimes of which they are the victim are dropped or dismissed even though related crimes continue to be prosecuted.

> In this regard, the usual methods of determining legislative intent produce inconsistent results. The law's sponsors explicitly advocated such a broad

> reading of the statute in the Senate floor debate. As Senator Kyl explained, subsection (e) employs "an intentionally broad definition because all victims of crime deserve to have their rights protected, *whether or not they are the victim of the count charged.*" Senate Debate at [150 *Cong. Rec.*] S4270 (statement of Sen. Kyl)(emphasis added); *id.* (statement of Sen. Feinstein agreeing with the same). On the other hand, the full Congress passed the bill knowing that similar language in an earlier victims' rights bill had been interpreted *not* to refer to uncharged conduct. In *Hughey v. United States*, 495 U.S. 411 (1990), the Supreme Court held that the 1982 Victim Witness Protection Act, 18 U.S.C. §3663(a)(2), authorized restitution only for loss caused by the specific conduct which forms the basis for the offense of conviction. Since the statute at issue in *Hughey* and the CVRA use similar definitions of "victim," it appears that the same reasoning would exclude victims of uncharged conduct from the class of those entitled to participatory rights under the new law. The latter view is bolstered by the House report on CVRA which explicitly noted that 18 U.S.C. 37871(a)(6) "makes no changes in the law with respect to restitution." H.R.Rep. 108-711 (2004). *United States v. Turner*, 367 F.Supp.2d 319, 326-27 (E.D.N.Y. 2005)(parallel citations omitted).

Restitution Case Law: Family of Homicide Victims

Like the restitution statutes, section 3771 states that in the case of a deceased victim, "the legal guardians of the crime victim or the representatives of the crime victim's estate, family members, or any other persons appointed as suitable by the court, *may assume the crime victim's rights.*" This suggests that family members of the deceased are not themselves considered victims. It implies that one of the parents and other relatives of an adult homicide victim may assume the victim's rights, but otherwise are entitled to none of the rights found in section 3771.

The restitution cases may lend some credence to this view.[32] Early case law construing section 3771 seems to leave the question unsettled. In discussing whether court appointment of a representative for a deceased "actual" victim was necessary, one court appears to have assumed that family members of a homicide victim are not themselves victims per se:

> *Persons Other Than Actual Victims...* Where the actual victim is deceased, a minor, incompetent, or incapacitated, "the legal guardians of the crime victim or the representatives of the crime victim's estate, family members, or any other persons appointed as suitable by the court, may assume the crime victim's rights under this chapter." 18 U.S.C. 3771(e). The provision appears to mean that where a surrogate is required and one is available, that

> person will automatically "assume the crime victim's rights" without the need for any action by the court. It is only where no such person can be identified — or, presumably, where any such person is unwilling or unable to assume that role — that a court need consider appointing a suitable surrogate. *United States v. Turner*, 367 F.Supp.2d 319, 329 (E.D.N.Y. 2005).

A second court conducting a the trial for the murders of Gregory Nicholson; Terry DeGeus; Lori, Amber and Kandi Duncan, observed:

> In this case, the government has identified the following "victim witnesses": Terry DeGeus's father, mother, sister, two brothers, ex-wife, and daughter; Lori Duncan's father, mother, brother and sister, who are, respectively Kandi and Amber Duncan's grandfather, grandmother, uncle and aunt; Kandi and Amber Duncan's father, other grandfather, and other grandmother; and Greg Nicholson's ex-wife, who is the mother of his children, and two daughters. Johnson does not dispute, and the court expressly finds, that each of these persons is either "a person directly and proximately harmed as a result of the commission of" one or more of the federal offenses charged against Johnson, that is, the murders of Greg Nicholson, Lori Duncan, Kandi Duncan, Amber Duncan, or Terry DeGeus, or that, owing to the deaths of these alleged murder victims in this case, the murder victims' family members identified by the government are "representatives of the crime victim's estate" or "family members." Therefore, these persons qualify for the rights afforded by §3771, *United States v. Johnson*, 362 F.Supp.2d 1043, 1055-56 (N.D. Iowa 2005).[33]

The Attorney General's *Guidelines* indicate that a family member, estate representative or court appointee may serve in the victim's stead in cases of death, infancy or incapacity, arguable implying that family members are not considered victims in their own right.[34]

Crimes under What Law

Various past proposed constitutional amendments would have covered the victims of crimes committed in violation of state law, the United States Code, the Code of Military Justice, the District of Columbia Code, and/or U.S. territorial codes.[35] Section 3771 is more modest. It applies to the victims harmed as a result of "the commission of a Federal offense or an offense in the District of Columbia."[36] It clearly does not apply to the victims of state crimes, unless the underlying misconduct also violates federal or D.C. law. The specific inclusion of only the District of Columbia in section 3771 in light of the specific inclusion of the territories in some of the past proposals to amend the Constitution might be seen as evidence that Congress did not intend section 3771 to cover victims of crimes committed in violation of the various territorial codes, which often have their own extensive victims' rights provisions.[37] By the same token, past attention to the victims of military offenses may suggest that section 3771 is not intended to cover the victims of violations of the Code of Military Justice.[38] On the other hand, the section apparently covers victims of juvenile delinquency with respect to misconduct that in the case of an adult offender would have been a violation of federal or D.C. law, although the availability of particular rights under section 3771 may depend upon whether the juvenile proceedings are open or closed.[39]

THE RIGHT TO BE REASONABLY PROTECTED FROM THE ACCUSED

> The right to be reasonably protected from the accused. 18 U.S.C. 3771(a)(1).

Section 3771 lists the right to be reasonably protected from the accused first among its victims rights. Most of section 3771's components can be traced to a comparable provision in the 108th Congress proposed constitutional amendments. This one is a little different. The constitutional amendment proposals spoke of a right to have judicial decisions made with an eye to victim safety.[40] The previous language focused on "adjudicative decisions;" the new language has no such limitation. The earlier language seemed to impose an obligation to guard against threats to victim safety, from whatever source; the new language establishes a right to the victim to be protected against the accused. Use of the term "accused" and portions of the scant legislative history might be read to imply that the right expires with the conviction of the accused at which point he would ordinarily be referred to as the offender.[41] Nevertheless the colloquy on the floor between two of the principal Senate sponsors ended with the comment that they considered the term "accused" in 3771 to mean "convicted" as well.[42] But earlier in their discussion, they summarized the right simply using a trial protection example.[43]

The clause appears to have been the subject of little, if any, judicial attention. One commentator has observed that "the legal significance, if any, of these general provisions is unclear."[44] At the very least, the section provides an explicit justification for compatible judicial action taken in the interest of victim safety.[45]

NOTICE

> The right to reasonable, accurate, and timely notice of any public court proceeding, or any parole proceeding, involving the crime or of any release or escape of the accused. 18 U.S.C. 3771(a)(2).
>
> Officers and employees of the Department of Justice and other departments and agencies of the United States engaged in the detection, investigation, or prosecution of crime shall make their best efforts to see that crime victims are notified of, and accorded, the rights described in subsection (a). . . Notice of release otherwise required pursuant to this chapter shall not be given if such notice may endanger the safety of any person. 18 U.S.C. 3771(c)(1),(3).
>
> In a case where the court finds that the number of crime victims makes it impracticable to accord all of the crime victims the rights described in subsection (a), the court shall fashion a reasonable procedure to give effect to this chapter that does not unduly complicate or prolong the proceedings. 18 U.S.C. 3771(d)(2).

Notice allows victims to assert their rights, facilitates their participation, assures them that justice is being done, and affords them the opportunity to take protective measures when the accused is at large.[46] Section 3771's notification rights are subject to several limitations, some explicit, some implicit. The section explicitly excuses a failure to notify victims of the release of an accused when to do so might be dangerous,[47] and it permits the courts to seek reasonable accommodations when the number of victims in a given case precludes strict compliance with the section's demands.[48]

The implicit limitation is constitutional. In some circumstances, the manner in which notice is provided may intrude upon the rights of the accused to an impartial jury trial or other constitutional rights of the accused.[49] Under such circumstances, the statutory rights of the victim must yield.

There is also an omission. Section 3771 does not give victims the right to notification of their rights; it merely imposes an obligation upon government officials to "make their best efforts to see that crime victims are notified" of them.[50]

This notification of the rights established was a component of the early constitutional amendment proposals,[51] which followed the lead of several state constitutions and statutes.[52] It was originally seen as a victim's counterpart to the

Miranda warnings enjoyed by an accused and as a prerequisite if the proposed amendments were to function effectively.[53] There were objections, however, that the warnings were out of character with the other rights conveyed by the Constitution and might pose implementation problems — objections that ultimately prevailed apparently,[54] since the provision was not included in later proposals.[55]

In this respect and others section 3771's notice clause, 18 U.S.C. 3771(a)(2), is essentially the same as its forerunner in the 108th Congress resolutions to amend the Constitution.[56] It differs slightly in that it makes special provisions for parole proceedings and insists that notice be "accurate" as well as "reasonable and timely." Moreover, unlike its predecessors, the clause is accompanied by language that imposes an obligation on the government to advise victims of their rights under the section and to inform them that they consult an attorney concerning those rights.[57]

The notice clause has several distinctive features:

- the notice rights apply only with respect to *public court proceedings* and *parole proceedings*;
- the rights attach to those proceedings *involving the crime* but not necessarily to all those related to the crime;
- victims are entitled to *reasonable, accurate and timely* notice; and
- victims are only entitled to notice of the release or escape of *the accused.*

Public Proceedings

The public proceedings limitation has been a feature of the victims rights proposals for some time. Speaking of the past constitutional proposals, Senate Judiciary Committee reports pointed out that:

Victims' rights under this provision are also limited to 'public proceedings.' Some proceedings, such as grand jury investigations, are not open to the public and accordingly would not be open to the victim. Other proceedings, while generally open, may be closed in some circumstances. For example, while plea proceedings are generally open to the public, a court might decide to close a proceeding in which an organized crime underling would plead guilty and agree to testify against his bosses. See 28 C.F.R. 50.9. Another example is provided by certain national security cases in which access to some proceedings can be restricted. See 'The Classified Information Procedures Act' 18 U.S.C. App.3. A victim would have no special right to attend. The amendment works no change in the standards for closing hearings, but rather simply recognizes that such nonpublic hearings take place. S.Rept. 108-191 at 34; *see also*, S.Rept. 106-254 at 30, S.Rept. 105-409 at 25.

When the proceedings are closed at the discretion of the court, however, the presence of the statutory rights may reinforce an inclination to nevertheless approve victim notification of their existence and outcome.[58]

Parole Proceedings

Congress abolished parole for those convicted of federal crimes committed after November 1, 1987, P.L. 98-473, 98 Stat. 2027 (1984). Parole is included in the sentencing regime relating to crimes committed in the District, D.C.CODE §§24-401 to 24-468.

Involving the Crime

The breadth of the phrase "*involving* the crime" used to describe the public proceedings covered by the notification right may raise questions too. The phrase clearly contemplates more than trial. Pre-trial and post-trial hearings involving motions to dismiss, to suppress evidence, to change venue, to grant a new trial, and any of the host of similar proceedings that flow to or from a criminal trial seem to come within the meaning of the term. The Senate reports' discussion of proceedings "*related to* the crime" in earlier versions, for instance, specifically mention appellate proceedings, S.Rept. 106-254 at 31, S.Rept.105-409 at 26.

The same reports indicate that at least at one time covered release proceedings were understood to include those involving "a release [from custody] of a defendant found not guilty of a crime by reason of insanity and then hospitalized in custody for further treatment," *Id.* at 36 and 30. Crime relatedness, understood in such terms, would presumably carry victim notice rights to a fairly wide range of civil and quasi-civil proceedings (e.g., habeas and civil forfeiture proceedings, and extradition hearings, to name but a few).

It may be for this reason that the phrase was changed to "involving the crime," a phrase that arguably imposes greater limits on the class of proceedings than might be considered "related," although not clearly sufficient to excuse notice of habeas, forfeiture, or the extradition proceedings.[59] Historical proposals were thought to perhaps embody notice rights for the victims of a defendant's past crimes, and victims of charges that had been dropped or dismissed, as well as victims of charges that had resulted in acquittal.[60] The change might be considered a repudiation of that construction as well.

The Senate Judiciary Committee, however, indicated that no such repudiation was intended in the case of the proposed constitutional amendment and stated simply that the "public proceedings are those 'relating to the crime,'" S.Rept. 108-191 at 34. In doing so, it might be thought to have embraced earlier descriptions of proceedings related to the crime, even though the Committee's examples in the 108th Congress were much more modest in some places, *id.* ("the right applies not only to initial hearings on a case, but also rehearings, hearing at an appellate level, and any case on a subsequent remand").[61] The colloquy on the floor between Senate sponsors of section 3771 is somewhat ambiguous but seems to confirm that the proceedings as to which notice is due include appellate proceedings.[62] By confining the proceedings covered to "court" and parole proceedings, section 3771 eliminates the speculation previously possible that the rights might be available in an administrative context such as in administrative immigration proceedings.

Reasonable, Accurate and Timely Notice

The inclusion of a "timeliness" requirement to the notice right seems significant, because it would appear to greatly reduce the prospect of "reasonable" but ineffective notice. Yet the Committee report issued after its addition in the constitutional amendment proposal makes no note of it and continues to describe the obligation in the same terms used prior to the change.[63] Under pre-addition proposals it was unclear whether reasonableness was to be judged by the level of official effort or by the effectiveness of the effort. The Senate reports noted that heroic efforts were not expected but due diligence was, S.Rept. 108-191 at 34; S.Rept. 106-254 at 30, S.Rept. 105-409 at 25. But the obvious purpose for the right to notice was to provide a gateway to the amendment's other rights. Even without the addition of the clarifying "timely" requirement, what was reasonable might have been judged by whether the efforts were calculated to permit meaningful exercise of the amendment's other rights.[64]

The Senate reports, however, explained that in rare circumstances notice by publication might be reasonable,[65] although if judged by existing due process standards such notice might not have been adequate in ordinary circumstances.[66] Notice given after a proceeding was conducted might have seemed unreasonable because the want of timely notice might constitute an effective exclusion from the proceedings or might defeat the right to make a victim impact statement.[67] The addition of a timeliness requirement seems to reduce the possibility of "reasonable" but untimely notification.[68] The same might be said for the new demand that notice be "accurate." It might seem difficult to imagine how notice could be considered either timely or reasonable, if for want of accuracy it effectively defeated a victim's opportunity to exercise his or her rights. One court has suggested that the "accuracy" modification was made to ensure that victims are kept advised of schedule changes.[69]

In the context of release notifications, the most vexing reasonableness questions may arise should the right extend both to the accused and to the convicted as discussed below. In some instances such as the right to notification of the release of prisoner following full service of his sentence, section 3771 may require notification of victims who would not previously have been entitled to notification and whose identity and location are therefore unknown to custodial authorities.[70]

Application may be challenging in the area of bail as well. The section grants both a right to consideration of the victim's safety and a right to reasonable notice, attendance, and comment. Under earlier circumstances it might not be unusual for an accused to be released on recognizance or bail before authorities could reasonably be expected to provide victims with timely notice. It may be that the section contemplates postponement of the accused's initial judicial appearance until after victims can be notified and can be given a reasonable period of time to prepare and present their views.

Early constitutional amendment proposals seemed to explicitly anticipate that a failure of timely notice in a bail context could be rectified by recourse to the provision in the amendment that permitted the bail decision to be revisited at the behest of a victim.[71] The section contains no such explicit provision, but nothing in the section precludes revisitation — other than abandonment of the earlier explicit provision perhaps.[72]

Release or Escape of the Accused

Section 3771 refers to notice of the release or escape of *the accused.* The implication is that there is no right to notice of a release or escape following conviction, since at that point the defendant is "convicted" rather than "accused." If this is the section's meaning, the consequences of the change are considerable. The administrative burdens associated with notifying victims every time an inmate is released from custody are not insignificant. This is especially true if the section is construed to apply to the future release or escape of prisoners convicted of crimes committed prior to its effective date.

Nevertheless, the Committee report in the 108th Congress suggests that in the equivalent language of the proposed constitutional amendment the Senate Judiciary Committee considered the terms "accused" and "convicted" interchangeable and intended no change from earlier more generously worded proposals:

> The release [which triggers a notification requirement] must be one "relating to the crime." This includes not only a release after a criminal conviction but also, for example, a release of a defendant found not guilty of a crime by reason of insanity and then hospitalized in custody for further treatment, or a release pursuant to a habitual sex offender statute, S.Rept. 108-191 at 35.
>
> The sponsors of section 3771 endorsed this view as well:
>
> Mrs. FEINSTEIN. . . One final point. Throughout this act, reference is made to the "accused." Would the Senator also agree that it is our intention to use this word in the broadest sense to include both those charged and convicted so that the rights we establish apply throughout the criminal justice system?
> Mr. KYL. Yes, that is it my understanding. 150 *Cong. Rec.* S4270 (daily ed. April 22, 2004).

Moreover, the section probably cannot fairly be read to cut off the rights it promises upon the return of a guilty verdict (when the defendant ceases to be an "accused" because of his conviction), since it grants victims explicit rights at sentencing, 18 U.S.C. 3771(a)(4), and at parole proceedings, 18 U.S.C. 3771(a)(2), (4).

The right may be limited under section 3771(c)(3) when notification would be dangerous.[73] The section's sponsors, however, urged that the limitation be invoked judiciously.[74]

Multiple Victims

Each of the rights found in section 3771(a), including the right to notice, is subject to a limitation when the court finds it impractical because of the sheer number of victims to fully accommodate them all, 18 U.S.C. 3771(d)(2). The provision has no predecessor in the constitutional amendment proposals. The Senate sponsors made it clear that they expected courts that find they must invoke the provision to develop alternative procedures to minimize the curtailment of rights.[75]

ATTENDANCE

> The right not to be excluded from any such public court proceeding, unless the court, after receiving clear and convincing evidence, determines that testimony by the victim would be materially altered if the victim heard other testimony at that proceeding. 18 U.S.C. 3771(a)(3).[76]

Section 3771 promises victims a limited attendance right, that is, a right not to be excluded from public court proceedings unless attendance would color their subsequent testimony.

The Constitution promises the accused a public trial by an impartial jury[77] and affords him the right to be present at all critical stages of the proceedings against him.[78] It offers victims no such prerogatives. Their status is at best that of any other member of the general public and, in fact, the Constitution screens the accused's right to an impartial jury trial from the overexuberance of the public.[79]

Moreover, victims are even more likely to be barred from the courtroom during trial than members of the general public. Ironically, the victim's status as a witness, the avenue of most likely access to pre-trial proceedings, is the very attribute most likely to result in exclusion from the trial.

Sequestration, or the practice of separating witnesses and holding outside the courtroom all but the witness on the stand, is of ancient origins and "consists merely in preventing one prospective witness from being taught by hearing another's testimony."[80] The principle has been embodied in Rule 615 of the Federal Rules of Evidence and in state rules that adopt the federal practice.[81]

Victims' advocates contend that it should be fundamental that individuals may attend all proceedings, particularly any trial, involving the crime visited upon them. Yet an absolute right to attend all proceedings may sometimes be unfair, and in some instances even a violation of due process or the right to trial by an impartial jury.

Section 3771 assures victims of the right not to be excluded from any public proceedings involving the crime except when to attend would color their subsequent testimony. It is one area where balancing the interests of victim, defendant, and government may be the most challenging.

The language used in section 3771's attendance right is comparable to that found in the earlier "best efforts" statute which recognizes the right of victims "to be present at all public court proceedings related to the offense, unless the court determines that testimony by the victim would be materially affected if the victim heard other testimony at trial," 42 U.S.C. 10606(b)(4)(2000 ed.). Section 3771 also operates in conjunction with 18 U.S.C. 3510 which declares that in federal capital cases, victims who attend a trial are not disqualified from appearing as witnesses at subsequent sentencing hearings absent a danger of unfair prejudice, jury confusion, of the jury being misled, or as constitutionally required.[82] In other federal criminal cases, victims may be excluded from trial only as constitutionally required, 18 U.S.C. 3510(a).

Section 3771 is more limited than the constitutional amendment proposals which with early exceptions afforded a general right not to be excluded.[83] It was suggested that the phrase "not to be excluded" in the amendment proposals was used to avoid the claims that the proposal would entitle victims to transportation to relevant proceedings or to have proceedings scheduled for their convenience or to free them from imprisonment to attend proceedings.[84] In this it would be unlike a defendant's right to attend. Yet like a defendant's right to attend, the use of the phrase has been thought to permit exclusion of the victim for disruptive behavior, excessive displays of emotion, and other forms of impropriety for which a defendant might be excluded.[85]

As in the case of notification, the legislative history of constitutional amendment proposals indicates that the section plays no role in what public proceedings can be closed even though that action denies victims notice, attendance and allocution rights.[86] It suggests that a victim has little ground to object if a decision is made to close a traditionally public proceeding.

On the other hand, the section conveying the right is reenforced by a later section in which the courts are instructed to make every effort to ensure the fullest possible victim attendance.[87] Together they require the trial attendance of victims unless the court "finds by clear and convincing evidence that it is highly likely, not merely possible, that the victim-witness will alter his or her testimony" if allowed to attend prior to testifying.[88]

PARTICIPATION

> The right to be reasonably heard at any public proceeding in the district court involving release, plea, sentencing, or any parole proceeding. 18 U.S.C. 3771(a)(4).[89]

Unlike the rights to notice and not to be excluded, the right to be heard is a right to participate. The section describes the proceedings at which it may be invoked with greater particularity, and here too limits application to reasonable participation in public court and parole proceedings. It does not on its face give victims the right to be heard in closed proceedings or to be heard on other pre-trial motions, at trial, perhaps on appeal, or with respect to related forfeiture or habeas proceedings. Nor does it explicitly give the victim the right to be heard in any particular form. It is in these respects and others very much like the amendment proposals in the 108th Congress.[90]

Reasonably Heard

The right to be reasonably heard raises three possible issues: (1) is it a right to comment or to command; (2) does the right include the right to select the method of communication — orally or in writing; and (3) are there limitations on the information the victim has right to convey. When the comment or command issue arose in connection with the proposed constitutional amendments, the Senate Judiciary Committee reports answered that the right was not a veto but an opportunity to present relevant information.[91] The later legislative history of section 3771 is silent on the question, but any contrary construction would appear to have constitutional implications.[92]

The evolution of the "reasonably heard" language complicates the method of communication issue. At one time, the proposed constitutional amendments spoke of a right to be "heard, if present, and to submit a statement."[93] When the phrase "if present, and to submit a statement" was dropped and the right defined as the right to be "reasonably heard," one hearing witness expressed concern that the courts would construe the new language to convey an absolute right to make an oral statement:

> I would expect courts to interpret the deletion of 'submit a statement' to signal a legislative intent to allow victims actually to be 'heard' by making an oral statement. Nor do I think the use of the term 'reasonably to be heard' would alter that interpretation; instead, I believe courts would likely reconcile the two changes by interpreting 'reasonably' to mean that a victim's oral statement could be subjected to reasonable time and subject matter restrictions. If the above is correct then prison officials might face an extremely burdensome choice of either transporting incarcerated victims to court for the purpose of being heard or providing for live transmissions to the court room.
>
> A related problem would extend beyond prison walls. Because the difference between the previous and current versions of the Amendment suggest that a victim must be allowed specifically to be "heard" rather than simply to "submit a statement", a victim might persuade a court that the "reasonable opportunity to be heard" guaranteed by the current version of the Amendment carries with it an implicit guarantee that the government will take affirmative steps, if necessary, to provide such a reasonable opportunity. This undermines the intent of the Amendment's careful use of negative phrasing with respect to the right not to be excluded from public proceedings — a formulation designed to avoid a government obligation to provide funding, to schedule the timing of a particular proceeding according to a victim wishes, or otherwise assert affirmative effort to make it possible for a victim to attend proceedings. *House Hearing V* at 79 (statement of James Orenstein).

The Senate Committee report specifically denied that the language in the proposed amendment was intended to create a right to transportation to the trial,[94] but this very point has already been a source of judicial division. One district court and one appellate panel believe that the right to be reasonably heard, at least at sentencing, gives the victim the right to make an oral statement;[95] at least in a bail context, another district court believes it includes no such right and that courts may limit the presentation to written presentations;[96] and in yet a third view, an uncertain member of the appellate panel suggests that reason may limit the right in some sentencing contexts.[97]

Nevertheless, it is certainly difficult to argue that the sponsors of section 3771 believed the right to be heard could be confined to a written statement, particularly at sentencing, in the absence of an overwhelming number of victims:

> This right of crime victims not to be excluded from the proceedings provides a foundation for the next section, section 2, (a)(4), which provides

> victims the right to reasonably be heard at any public proceeding involving release, plea, or sentencing. *This provision is intended to allow crime victims to directly address the court in person.* It is not necessary for the victim to obtain the permission of either party to do so. This right is a right independent of the government or the defendant that allows the victim to address the court. To the extent the victim has the right to independently address the court, the victim acts as a in independent participant in the proceedings. 150 *Cong.Rec.* S4268 (daily ed. April 22, 2004)(remarks of Sen. Kyl)(emphasis added).

As to the content of the victim's communication, the legislative history is sparse. The Committee reports on the proposed amendments speak of the courts' discretion to reasonable limit the length and content of the victim's communication.[98] Hearing witnesses opined that the right in the proposed amendment embodied the right "to make a recommendation regarding the appropriate sentence to be imposed, including in capital cases."[99] The clearest statement of intent comes from the Senate colloquy, "When a victim invokes this right during plea and sentencing proceedings, it is intended that [] he or she be allowed to provide all three types of victim impact — the character of the victim, the impact of the crime on the victim, the victim's family and the community, and sentencing recommendations."[100]

Public Court Release Proceedings

From the beginning, the amendment proposals and section 3771 have spoken of the right to be heard in "release" proceedings.[101] There seems to be little dispute that the term contemplates the right to be heard at bail proceedings. What other proceedings, if any, the term encompasses is a question complicated by the qualifiers with which successive proposals surrounded the release-related right.

Past amendment proposals once conveyed a right to be heard at public proceedings relating to a *conditional* release from custody and, to the extent the inmate enjoyed a right to be heard, at closed parole hearings.[102] Later versions simply conveyed a right to be heard at public release proceedings.[103] The clear implication was that under the later proposals victims had no right to be heard at closed parole hearings, regardless of whether the inmate had a right to be heard.[104] On the other hand, the new formulation seemed to open a wider range of proceedings to victim allocution.

There was always some ambiguity over whether conditional release proceedings meant proceedings where release might be granted if certain conditions were met *before* release, like acquittal at trial, or proceedings where release bound the accused or convicted offender to honor certain conditions *after* release, like bail, or both. In any event, in bygone proposals the Senate Judiciary Committee read "conditional" in the phrase "*conditional* release *from custody*," as a word of limitation:

> The amendment extends the right to be heard to proceedings determining a '*conditional* release' from custody. This phrase encompasses, for example, hearings to determine any pretrial or posttrial release (including comparable releases during or after an appeal) on bail, personal recognizance, to the custody of a third person, or under any other conditions, including pretrial diversion programs. Other examples of conditional release include work release and home detention. Its also includes parole hearings or their functional equivalent, both because parole hearings have some discretion in releasing offenders and because releases from prison are typically subject to various conditions such as continued good behavior. It would also include a release from a secure mental facility for a criminal defendant or one acquitted on the grounds of insanity. A victim would not have a right to speak, by virtue of this amendment, at a hearing to determine "unconditional" release. For example, a victim could not claim a right to be heard at a hearing to determine the jurisdiction of the court or compliance with the governing statute of limitations, even though a finding in favor of the defendant on these points might indirectly and ultimately lead to the 'release' of the defendant. Similarly, there is no right to be heard when a prisoner is released after serving the statutory maximum penalty, or the full term of his sentence. There would be proceeding to "determine"a release in such situations and the release would also be without condition if the court's authority over the prisoner had expired. S.Rept.106-254 at 32; S.Rept. 105-409 at 27.

Thus by removing the words "conditional" and "from custody," the proposals and consequently section 3771 perhaps should be understood to allow victims the right to be heard on most pre-trial motions as well as most post-trial, pre- appellate petitions, or at least any that might result in a release of the accused or the convicted offender from jeopardy. For example, it might support an argument that the section gives victims the right be heard at trial by the trier of fact (judge or jury) on whether the defendant should or should not be convicted on any of the charges at issue (i.e., at least limited trial participation, although the Committee report denied any such intent).[105]

It may seem more logical to suggest that proceedings to which the right attaches are only those where the issue of whether the defendant should be released is squarely addressed — bail proceedings and habeas proceedings under 28 U.S.C. 2255 — and not proceedings where the issues addressed may be resolved in a manner that leads the defendant's release. Yet at least one commentator has suggested that the right to be heard in release proceedings includes the right to be heard upon motions to dismiss charges. The comment comes in a discussion of the changes in the Federal Rules of Criminal Procedure appropriate to implement the section. Under one such proposed change, the court would be required to consider the views of the victim before it ruled on a motion to dismiss charges, a "proposed change [which] would implement a victim's right to be 'treated with fairness' and to be heard at any proceeding 'involving release' of the defendant."[106] The same logic would appear to support a victim's right to be heard in suppression hearings and other pre-trial motions.

Regardless of how expansively "release" is construed, there are some proceedings that seem beyond the scope of section 3771's participation rights. The right attaches to public proceedings. In theory therefore, it does not apply in grand jury proceedings or proceedings such as those involving juveniles which are closed at the discretion of the court.[107] The right attaches to public proceedings "in the district court." In theory therefore, it does not apply in appellate proceedings whether relating to bail or otherwise.[108]

Even where the right appears to otherwise apply on its face, some courts may be reluctant to postpone the defendant's initial appearance or release hearings to fully accommodate the right.[109]

Plea Bargains

Victims have a special interest in the right to be heard before the court accepts a plea agreement. Negotiated guilty pleas account for over ninety percent of the criminal convictions obtained.[110] Plea bargaining offers the government convictions without the time, cost, or risk of a trial, and in some cases a defendant turned cooperative witness. It offers a defendant conviction but on less serious charges, and/or with the expectation of a less severe sentence than if he or she were convicted following a criminal trial,[111] and/or the prospect of other advantages controlled, at least initially by the prosecutor — agreements not to prosecute family members or friends, or to prosecute them on less serious charges than might otherwise be filed;[112] forfeiture concessions;[113] testimonial immunity;[114] entry into a witness protection program;[115] and informant's rewards,[116] to mention a few.

For the victim, a plea bargain may come as an unpleasant surprise, one that may jeopardize the victim's prospects for restitution; one that may result in a sentence the victim finds insufficient;[117] and/or one that changes the legal playing field so that the victim has become the principal target of prosecution.[118]

Section 3771 assures crime victims of the right to reasonably be heard at proceedings when a plea bargain is accepted. The right only attaches to the acceptance of plea bargains in open court (i.e., at public proceedings).[119] The right clearly does not vest a victim with the right to participate in plea negotiations between the defendant and the prosecutor, which are neither public nor proceedings.[120] By the same token, the right to be heard is not the right to decide; victims must be heard, but their views are not necessarily controlling.[121] It remains to be seen whether the existence of the right in open court will lead to more proceedings being closed to avoid the complications of recognizing the right.

Sentencing

At common law, victims had no right to address the court before sentence was imposed upon a convicted defendant. The victim's right to bring the impact of the crime upon him to the attention of the court was one of the early goals of the victims' rights efforts. The Supreme Court has struggled with the propriety of victim impact statements in the context of capital punishment cases, ultimately concluding that they pose no necessary infringement upon the rights of the accused.[122] In doing so, it noted:

> Our holding today is limited to the ["wrongly decided"] holdings of *Booth v. Maryland*, 482 U.S. 496 (1987), and *South Carolina v. Gathers*, 490 U.S. 805 (1989), that evidence and argument relating to the victim and the impact of the victim's death on the victim's family are inadmissible at a capital sentencing hearing. *Booth* also held that the admission of a victim's family members' characterizations and opinions about the crime, the defendant, and the appropriate sentence violates the Eighth Amendment. No evidence of the latter sort was presented at the trial in this case. *Payne v. Tennessee*, 501 U.S. 808, 830 n.2 (1991).

The federal courts have concluded from this that in capital cases victim impact statements are constitutionally precluded from including "characterizations and opinions about the crime, the defendant, and the appropriate sentence."[123] Constitutionally grounded the proscription remains in effect, the provisions of section 3771 notwithstanding.

In cases not capital, as noted earlier, the sponsors of the legislation seem to have anticipated that the right included the right to be heard orally and did not intend to permit the courts to require participation in writing except by operation of section 3771(d)(2) when faced with an overwhelming number of victims at the sentencing of single defendant. Thus far, the courts seem to concur.[124]

Parole and Pardon

Section 3771 gives victims the right to be heard at parole proceedings. As noted earlier, parole is not part of the federal criminal justice process relating to any crime committed after November 1, 1987, but continues to be a feature of the District of Columbia criminal justice process.[125]

The constitutional amendment proposals in the 108th Congress provided victims with a right to be heard at public pardons proceedings. Section 3771 has no such provision. The right to be reasonably heard applies to public court proceedings. The Constitution vests the pardoning power in the President[126] and the power is exercised through an administrative process that does not involve public court proceedings.[127] Under section 3771(a)(2), however, should a prisoner be pardoned and consequently released his victims would be entitled to notice.

Appeals

Section 3371 rather clearly implies that victims have no right to be heard on appeal other than through mandamus. The right to be heard is couched in terms that limit both the forum ("in district court") and the proceedings ("release, plea, sentencing or any parole"). Moreover, elsewhere the government is entrusted with responsibility to espouse the victim's rights on appeal, apparently as a matter of discretion.[128]

CONFER

> The reasonable right to confer with the attorney for the Government in the case. 18 U.S.C. 3771(a)(5).

This is a right not found in the constitutional amendment proposals. The statute might be read to afford a right to confer beginning with the commission of the offense, including with regard to the manner in which the investigation is conducted and the decision as to what charges to bring and against whom. The Senate sponsors of the section, however, described an extensive but more limited right:

> Section 2, (a)(5) provides a right to confer with the attorney for the Government in the case. This right is intended to be expansive. For example. the victim has the right to confer with the Government concerning any critical stage or disposition of the case. The right, however, is not limited to these examples. I ask the Senator if he concurs in this intent.
> Mr. KYL. Yes. The intent of this section is just as the Senator says. This right to confer does not give the crime victim any right to direct the prosecution. Prosecutors should consider it part of their profession to be available to consult with crime victims about the concerns the victims may have which are pertinent to the case, case proceedings or dispositions. Under this provision, victims are able to confer with the Government's attorney about proceedings *after charging*. 150 *Cong. Rec.* S4268 (daily ed. April 22, 2004)(remarks of Sens. Feinstein and Kyl)(emphasis added).

At least some courts appear to believe that exercise of the right must be self-initiated.[129]

RESTITUTION

> The right to full and timely restitution as provided in law. 18 U.S.C. 3771(a)(6).

Like many other elements of section 3771, the language of this right is reminiscent of the constitutional amendment proposals in the 108th and 107th Congresses which spoke of a right "to full and timely restitution."[130] Those proposals were very different from earlier proposals. They did not establish a right to restitution in so many words. They did not explicitly convey a right to have proceedings reopened for failure to accommodate a victim's right to restitution. Instead for the first time they spoke of just and timely claims to restitution, two concepts which could be subject to several interpretations.

The first victims' rights proposals promised either a right "to an order of restitution from the convicted offender,"[131] or a right "to full restitution from the convicted offender."[132] Subsequent proposals opted for the right to an order version.[133] The proposals appeared to make restitution orders mandatory as a matter of right. The scope of the right was unstated.

Although the proposals applied to juvenile proceedings, the use of the term "convicted offender" might have been construed to limit their restitution command to criminal convictions and therefore not reach findings of delinquency.[134]

Restitution orders in a nominal amount or subject to priorities for criminal fines or forfeiture or other claims against the defendant's assets might have seemed inconsistent with the decision to elevate mandatory victim restitution to a constitutional right. Their legislative history indicated that these early proposals did "not confer on victims any rights to a specific amount of restitution, leaving the court free to order nominal restitution . . . . The right conferred on victims [was] one to an 'order' of restitution. With the order in hand, questions of enforcement of the order and its priority as against other judgments [were] left to the applicable Federal and State law," S.Rept. 106-254 at 37; S.Rept. 105-409 at 31.

The Committee reports, however, continuously suggested that the right might include the right to a pre-trial restraining order to prevent an accused from dissipating assets that might be used to satisfy a restitution order, S.Rept. 108-191 at 41; S.Rept. 106-254 at 37; S.Rept. 105-409 at 32. The right also might have extended to prevent dissipation in the form of payment of attorneys' fees for the accused, since the accused has only a qualified right to the assistance of counsel of his choice.[135]

What was a right to a restitution order prior to the 107th Congress became the right to consideration of just and timely victims' claims, appropriate to the circumstances, weighed against the interests of others, and perhaps only applicable during proceedings on other matters. At first glance, it appeared that as long as the victim's interest in just restitution when asserted in a timely manner was recognized, the amendment proposals left the law of restitution unchanged.

Not everyone read it that way. One commentator offered an example to illustrate his more expansive understanding of its reach:

> Jane Doe was beaten and raped in a remote wooded area of Vermont. . . . Her injuries were extensive.... When her case was resolved by way of a plea bargain she was not given the right to speak before the court. Incredibly, the sentence imposed did not order the criminal to pay restitution. Today he earns $7.50 an hour making furniture inside the prison walls — and none of it goes to her for her damages and injuries because it was not part of the criminal sentence. If this provision had been the law, Jane would today be receiving restitution payments each month. *House Hearing IV* at 27 (statement of Steven J. Twist).

The implication was that in horrific cases, victims had a right to restitution without reference to any other factors. Yet insertion of the word "just" for the first time in the restitution component of the amendment proposal presumably called for consideration of such factors when appropriate. Moreover, it probably precluded restitution claims by the "ripped-off" drug dealer or others victimized in the course of their own illegal conduct at least in some circumstances.[136]

Historic proposals explicitly allowed victims to reopen final proceedings in vindication of their right to restitution. That language disappeared and in its place was a reference to "timely" claims to restitution. The implications were obvious, but the statement quoted above seems to suggest that "timeliness" may be judged by the date of the injury, the date of sentencing, or the date on which the offender had the resources to begin paying restitution.

Section 3771 adds the phrase "as provided in law" to the right and substitutes "full and timely" restitution for "just and timely" restitution. With the changes, the section seems to confirm rather than enlarge existing law in the area of restitution. Sponsors felt that elsewhere the section bolsters the victim's restitution interest by ensuring the victim's rights to notice, consultation and participation.[137] One appellate court has pointed out that the promise of "full" restitution extends only as far as the law provides, a fact that "makes it clear that Congress recognized that there would be numerous situations when it would be impossible for multiple crime victims to the same set of crimes to be repaid every dollar they had lost."[138]

REASONABLE FREEDOM FROM DELAY

> The right to proceedings free from unreasonable delay. 18 U.S.C. 3771(a)(7)

The United States Constitution guarantees those accused of a federal crime a speedy trial;[139] the due process clause of the Fourteenth Amendment makes the right binding upon the states,[140] whose constitutions often have a companion provision.[141] The constitutional right is reenforced by statute and rule in the form of speedy trial laws in both the federal and state realms.[142]

"Ironically, however, the defendant is often the only person involved in a criminal proceeding without an interest in a prompt trial. Delay often works to the defendant's advantage. Witnesses may become unavailable, their memories may fade, evidence may be lost, changes in the law may be beneficial, or the case may simply receive a lower priority with the passage of time."[143]

Until recently, victims had no comparable rights, although their advocates contended they had a very real interest in prompt disposition. Some victims sought to put a traumatic episode behind them; some wanted to see justice done quickly; some hoped simply to end the trail of inconveniences and hardship that all too often fell to their lot as witnesses.[144]

A few states have since enacted statutory or constitutional provisions establishing a victim's right to "prompt" or "timely" disposition of the case in one form or another.[145] The federal statutory victims' bill of rights, 42 U.S.C. 10606 (2000 ed.), did not include a speedy trial provision, but Congress has encouraged the states to include a right to a reasonably expeditious trial among the rights they afford victims.[146]

Section 3771(a)(7) seems to convey a more generous right than its predecessors in the proposed constitutional amendments. Yet in spite of what might appear to be an evolutionary development, the right has been described at each stage in much the same terms; throughout the years it was suggested that perhaps the standards used to judge the defendant's constitutional speedy trial right govern here as well.[147]

In the beginning, proposals sometimes actually spoke of a victims' *speedy trial* right,[148] and in other instances preferred to describe it as the right to have "*proceedings* resolved in a prompt and timely manner."[149] Proposals in the 105th Congress continued the split, some focused on the beginning and completion of trial; others on a finality of the proceedings.[150] In the following Congress, the proposals all called for "consideration of the victim's interest in a *trial* free from unreasonable delay."[151] In this form, the right was one relevant only in a trial and pre-trial context. The proposals seemed to carry the implication that the right could only be claimed in conjunction with other proceedings (e.g., "considered" in the context of a defense or government motion for a continuance but not a defendant's motion for a new trial), but not necessarily provide grounds for a free standing victim's motion when the question of timing was not otherwise before the court.

In the 108th Congress the formulation referred to "the right to adjudicative decisions that duly consider the victim's ... interest in avoiding unreasonable delay."[152] Some of the words were new. The phrase "adjudicative decisions" replaced "trials" and "proceedings"; "duly consider" appeared instead of "consideration"; and "avoiding unreasonable delay" stood where "free from unreasonable delay" once was. Yet at least some of the concepts seemed to remand constant. Reasonable delays were to countenanced; unreasonable delays tolerated only if they are outweighed by other interests. The Supreme Court's speedy trial jurisprudence was to be used as a guide for what was reasonable.[153]

On the other hand, the new wording left other questions unanswered. Were victims to have the right to be heard prior to any decision that might either cause or reduce delay? One hearing witness expressed concern that the right to consideration of the interest might include the right to voice the interest on questions other than scheduling: "Does a crime victim have the right to object to the admission of evidence on the ground that it might lengthen the trial?" *House Hearing V* at 81 (statement of James Orenstein). Yet, the amendment's language did not necessarily create a right to assert the interest. The delay avoidance interest triggered a right to consideration. Interests elsewhere in the amendment triggered a right to be heard. And the right to be heard related to matters of "public release, plea, sentencing, reprieve, and pardon proceedings," not to the matters of scheduling, motions, and other pre-trial and trial proceedings which were just as likely to produce delay. Courts might have concluded the differences were significant.

Section 3771(a)(7) continues to describe the right to delay avoidance in limiting terms, but apparently more expansively than its forebears: "the right to proceedings free from unreasonable delay." Its sponsors suggested than the right was aimed at scheduling delays particularly:

> I would like to move on to section 2, with a right to proceedings free from unreasonable delay. This provision does not curtail the government's need for reasonable time to organize and prosecute its case. Nor is the provision intended to infringe on the defendant's due process right to prepare a defense. Too often, however, delays in criminal proceedings occur for the mere convenience of the parties and those delays reach beyond the time needed for defendant's due process or the government's need to prepare. The result of such delays is that victims cannot begin to put the crime behind them and they continue to be victimized. It is not right to hold crime victims under the stress and pressure of future court proceedings merely because it is convenient for the parties or the court.
>
> This provision should be interpreted so that the any decision to continue a criminal case should include reasonable consideration of the rights under this section.150 *Cong.Rec.* S4268-269 (daily ed. April 22, 2004).

Early case law indicates that the courts are sensitive to victims' interest in delay avoidance,[154] but also that in some instances delay may be in the interest of at least some victims.[155]

Fairness, Dignity, and Privacy

> The right to be treated with fairness and with respect for the victim's dignity and privacy. 18 U.S.C. 3771(a)(8)

This right rarely found explicit expression in the proposed constitutional amendments, although it clearly lies at the heart of all of them. The same language appears in the earlier federal "best efforts" statute, 42 U.S.C. 10606 (2000 ed.), and a similar right is featured in many of the state constitutional and statutory victims rights provisions.[156]

Responsibilities of the Courts

> In any court proceeding involving an offense against a crime victim, the court shall ensure that the crime victim is afforded the rights described in subsection (a). Before making a determination described in subsection (a)(3), the court shall make every effort to permit the fullest attendance possible by the victim and shall consider reasonable alternatives to the exclusion of the victim from the criminal proceeding. The reasons for any decision denying relief under this chapter shall be clearly stated on the record. 18 U.S.C. 3771(b).

This section is new. None of the proposed constitutional amendments featured an equivalent. It has no counterpart in the earlier federal "best efforts" section, 42 U.S.C. 10606 (2000 ed.). At least one court has expressed the view that "the provision requires at least some proactive procedure designed to ensure victims' rights," while noting the apparent primacy of the right to attend.[157] The trial court's obligation to "ensure" victims rights seems to set its responsibilities a notch above the "best efforts" level of obligation imposed upon other officials.[158]

RESPONSIBILITIES OF OTHER AUTHORITIES

Officers and employees of the Department of Justice and other departments and agencies of the United States engaged in the detection, investigation, or prosecution of crime shall make their best efforts to see that crime victims are *notified of, and* accorded, the rights described in subsection (a). 18 U.S.C. 3771(c)(1)(emphasis added).

The prosecutor shall advise the crime victim that the crime victim can seek the advice of an attorney with respect to the rights described in subsection (a). 18 U.S.C. 3771(c)(2).

Section 3771(c)(1) replicates the language of 42 U.S.C. 10606(a)(2000 ed.) with the addition of the notification in italics above. Section 3771(c)(2) is new and was added in recognition of the fact that the interests of the government and the interests of the victim may not always coincide.[159] None of the proposed constitutional amendments had a provision comparable to either section 3771(c)(1) or 3771(c)(2).

ENFORCEMENT

Who

> The crime victim or the crime victim's lawful representative, and the attorney for the Government may assert the rights described in subsection (a). . . 18 U.S.C. 3771(d)(1).
>
> In any appeal in a criminal case, the Government may assert as error the district court's denial of any crime victim's right in the proceeding to which the appeal relates. 18 U.S.C. 3771(d)(4).

Section 3771(d)(1) is an expansion of the related proposals contained in the proposed constitutional amendments. They contained an exclusive provision and made no mention of governmental representation (e.g., "Only the victim or the victim's lawful representative may assert the rights established by this article, and no person accused of the crime may obtain any form of relief hereunder"), S.J.Res.1/ H.J.Res. 48 (108th Cong.). Section 3771(d)(1) expressly authorizes the government to assert rights on behalf of the victim. Moreover, it is not exclusive. It seems open to the possibility that the rights may asserted by someone other than the mentioned claimants — victims, victims' representatives and the government — as long as the claimant is not a defendant accused of the crime. The legislative history confirms the impression that "representatives" include both victims' attorneys and those standing in the stead of a legally unavailable victim; and it negates somewhat the implication that anyone other than the actual victim enjoys ultimate control of the victim's rights.[160] Some of the cases have already noted the propriety of prosecutors asserting victims' rights.[161]

The government's prerogative to assert the rights of a victim apparently includes the right to petition for mandamus when they are denied.[162]

Mandamus and Appeal

The rights described in subsection (a) shall be asserted in the district court in which a defendant is being prosecuted for the crime or, if no prosecution is underway, in the district court in the district in which the crime occurred. The district court shall take up and decide any motion asserting a victim's right forthwith. If the district court denies the relief sought, the movant may petition the court of appeals for a writ of mandamus. The court of appeals may issue the writ on the order of a single judge pursuant to circuit rule or the Federal Rules of Appellate Procedure. The court of appeals shall take up and decide such application forthwith within 72 hours after the petition has been filed. In no event shall proceedings be stayed or subject to a continuance of more than five days for purposes of enforcing this chapter. If the court of appeals denies the relief sought, the reasons for the denial shall be clearly stated on the record in a written opinion. 18 U.S.C. 3771(d)(3).

This provision originates in section 3771. It is more explicit than any of the proposed amendments. Furthermore it contemplates interlocutory appeals with stays or continuances of pending criminal proceedings of no more than five days, 18 U.S.C. 3771(d)(3). Early constitutional amendment proposals limited the use of stays[163] and later proposals were simply silent on the issue.[164]

The section's Senate sponsors apparently saw the availability of mandamus as a means of appellate review.[165] In other contexts it is more limited; it is a "drastic and extraordinary remedy reserved for really extraordinary cases."[166] The Second Circuit has observed that a mandamus "petitioner must usually demonstrate: (1) presence of a novel and significant question of law; (2) the inadequacy of other available remedies; and (3) the presence of a legal issue whose resolution will aid in the administration of justice."[167] It felt, however, that since Congress had designated mandamus as the principal avenue of review, it did not intend to require victims to "overcome the hurdles typically faced by a petitioner seeking review of a district court determination through a writ of mandamus."[168] Using for guidance the Supreme Court's determination of the appropriate standard of review under the Equal Access to Justice Act which grants attorneys' fees to the victims of governmental overreaching, the Circuit panel settled on an abuse of discretion standard.[169] The Ninth Circuit agreed.[170]

LIMITATIONS

Limits on Mandamus

> In no case shall a failure to afford a right under this chapter provide grounds for a new trial. A victim may make a motion to re-open a plea or sentence only if — (A) the victim has asserted the right to be heard before or during the proceeding at issue and such right was denied; (B) the victim petitions the court of appeals for a writ of mandamus within 10 days; and (C) in the case of a plea, the accused has not pled to the highest offense charged. This paragraph does not affect the victim's right to restitution as provided in title 18, United States Code. 18 U.S.C. 3771(d)(5).

Proponents of the proposed constitutional amendment wrestled with the question of the circumstances, if any, under which criminal proceedings could be reopened to correct a denial of a victim's rights. At first, they suggested that relief could only granted prospectively, specific judicial decisions could not be postponed or reopened.[171] Later, they yielded a bit and allowed bail and restitution proceedings to be revisited, but otherwise made the prospective nature of relief even more explicit.[172] Finally, they simply left the question for legislative resolution except for a prohibition on new trials.[173]

Section 3771(d)(5) limits the opportunity to revisit plea and sentencing proceedings. It says nothing about bail, restitution, or other trial proceedings, all of which are thus presumably subject to the expedited, five-day stay, mandamus procedure of section 3771(d)(3).

No New Rights for the Accused

> A person accused of the crime may not obtain any form of relief under this chapter. 18 U.S.C. 3771(d)(1).

Some of the constitutional amendment proposals relied on an assertion that "only" a victim or her representative could claim their benefits,[174] but most included an explicit disclaimer in one form or another that bar defendant's use of the proposed amendment.[175] The provision's intent is apparent and sparked little debate over the course of its legislative history.[176] Use of the term "the crime" seems to suggest that the disqualification is itself limited; an individual accused or convicted of one crime may none the less be the victim of another. This would appear to be so even if the two offenses arose out of the same event, such as a case of domestic violence in which each of the participants assaulted the other.

> In no case shall a failure to afford a right under this chapter provide grounds for a new trial ... 18 U.S.C. 3771(d)(5).

A similar clause appears in the proposed constitutional amendments,[177] but on a different footing. But for the clause in a constitutional amendment, a victim's right to attend trial might be thought to trump the constitutional protection of the accused against double jeopardy. On the other hand, the absence of such a clause in a statute such as section 3771 might be construed to mean that the new trial remedy would only be available to a victim if it were of benefit to the accused. If the accused had been acquitted double jeopardy would bar a new trial; if he had been convicted a new trial would afford him a second chance at acquittal.[178]

Many Victims — One Accused

> In a case where the court finds that the number of crime victims makes it impracticable to accord all of the crime victims the rights described in subsection (a), the court shall fashion a reasonable procedure to give effect to this chapter that does not unduly complicate or prolong the proceedings. 18 U.S.C. 3771(d)(2).

Section 3771(d)(2) has no counterpart in any of the proposed constitutional amendments. The committee reports accompanying the amendments did acknowledge that the right to "reasonable" notice might be honored less thoroughly in cases involving hundreds of victims than in cases involving only a few.[179] The same might have been said (but was not) of the right to be "reasonable" heard and the right not to be excluded. The amendments instead afforded the courts flexibility to deal with cases involving hundreds of victims or other unusual circumstances.[180] Section 3771(d)(2) deals with the challenge more explicitly, although both the language used and the legislative history make it clear that when necessary to invoke the section the courts are expected to adopt alternative procedures in the spirit of the reduced right.[181]

No Damages

> Nothing in this chapter shall be construed to authorize a cause of action for damages or to create, to enlarge, or to imply any duty or obligation to any victim or other person for the breach of which the United States or any of its officers or employees could be held liable in damages. Nothing in this chapter shall be construed to impair the prosecutorial discretion of the Attorney General or any officer under his direction. 18 U.S.C. 3771(d)(6).

The constitutional amendment proposals generally included a similar ban on damages.[182] They were thought to not only to bar a cause of action for damages on behalf of aggrieved victims but also to preclude requests for the appointment of counsel to represent indigent victims or for payment of attorneys fees for retained counsel.[183] The sponsors of section 3771 made no similar statements during the course of debate, but did point out that other sections of the legislation established a grant program to provide victims with legal assistance.[184] Other Members bemoaned the fact that the section makes no provision for the appointment of counsel for indigent victims.[185]

JUSTICE DEPARTMENT REGULATIONS

> Not later than 1 year after the date of enactment of this chapter, the Attorney General of the United States shall promulgate regulations to enforce the rights of crime victims and to ensure compliance by responsible officials with the obligations described in law respecting crime victims. 18 U.S.C. 3771(f)(1).

The Attorney General's regulations required by section 3771 must include the designation of an official to receive victim complaints concerning performance under the section, training for Justice Department employees, and disciplinary sanctions for willful and wanton violations, 18

U.S.C. 3771(f)(2). The Department of Justice issued revised victim assistance guidelines in May 2005 that include section 3771 matters.[186]

18 U.S.C. 3771 (TEXT)

(a) Rights of crime victims. — A crime victim has the following rights:

(1) The right to be reasonably protected from the accused.
(2) The right to reasonable, accurate, and timely notice of any public court proceeding, or any parole proceeding, involving the crime or of any release or escape of the accused.
(3) The right not to be excluded from any such public court proceeding, unless the court, after receiving clear and convincing evidence, determines that testimony by the victim would be materially altered if the victim heard other testimony at that proceeding.
(4) The right to be reasonably heard at any public proceeding in the district court involving release, plea, sentencing, or any parole proceeding.
(5) The reasonable right to confer with the attorney for the Government in the case.
(6) The right to full and timely restitution as provided in law.
(7) The right to proceedings free from unreasonable delay.
(8) The right to be treated with fairness and with respect for the victim's dignity and privacy.

(b) Rights afforded. — In any court proceeding involving an offense against a crime victim, the court shall ensure that the crime victim is afforded the rights described in subsection (a). Before making a determination described in subsection (a)(3), the court shall make every effort to permit the fullest attendance possible by the victim and shall consider reasonable alternatives to the exclusion of the victim from the criminal proceeding. The reasons for any decision denying relief under this chapter shall be clearly stated on the record.

(c) Best efforts to accord rights. —

(1) Government. — Officers and employees of the Department of Justice and other departments and agencies of the United States engaged in the detection, investigation, or prosecution of crime shall make their best efforts to see that crime victims are notified of, and accorded, the rights described in subsection (a).
(2) Advice of attorney. — The prosecutor shall advise the crime victim that the crime victim can seek the advice of an attorney with respect to the rights described in subsection (a).
(3) Notice. — Notice of release otherwise required pursuant to this chapter shall not be given if such notice may endanger the safety of any person.

(d) Enforcement and limitations. —

(1) Rights. — The crime victim or the crime victim's lawful representative, and the attorney for the Government may assert the rights described in subsection (a). A person accused of the crime may not obtain any form of relief under this chapter.
(2) Multiple crime victims. — In a case where the court finds that the number of crime victims makes it impracticable to accord all of the crime victims the rights described in subsection (a), the court shall fashion a reasonable procedure to give effect to this chapter that does not unduly complicate or prolong the proceedings.
(3) Motion for relief and writ of mandamus. — The rights described in subsection (a) shall be asserted in the district court in which a defendant is being prosecuted for the crime or, if no prosecution is underway, in the district court in the district in which the crime occurred. The district court shall take up and decide any motion asserting a victim's right forthwith. If the district court denies the relief sought, the movant may petition the court of appeals for a writ of mandamus. The court of appeals may issue the writ on the order of a single judge pursuant to circuit rule or the Federal Rules of Appellate Procedure. The court of appeals shall take up and decide such application forthwith within 72 hours after the petition has been filed. In no event shall proceedings be stayed or subject to a continuance of more than five days for purposes of enforcing this chapter. If the court of appeals denies the relief sought, the

reasons for the denial shall be clearly stated on the record in a written opinion.

(4) Error. — In any appeal in a criminal case, the Government may assert as error the district court's denial of any crime victim's right in the proceeding to which the appeal relates.

(5) Limitation on relief. — In no case shall a failure to afford a right under this chapter provide grounds for a new trial. A victim may make a motion to re-open a plea or sentence only if —

(A) the victim has asserted the right to be heard before or during the proceeding at issue and such right was denied;

(B) the victim petitions the court of appeals for a writ of mandamus within 10 days; and

(C) in the case of a plea, the accused has not pled to the highest offense charged.

This paragraph does not affect the victim's right to restitution as provided in title 18, United States Code.

(6) No cause of action. — Nothing in this chapter shall be construed to authorize a cause of action for damages or to create, to enlarge, or to imply any duty or obligation to any victim or other person for the breach of which the United States or any of its officers or employees could be held liable in damages. Nothing in this chapter shall be construed to impair the prosecutorial discretion of the Attorney General or any officer under his direction.

(e) Definitions. — For the purposes of this chapter, the term "crime victim" means a person directly and proximately harmed as a result of the commission of a Federal offense or an offense in the District of Columbia. In the case of a crime victim who is under 18 years of age, incompetent, incapacitated, or deceased, the legal guardians of the crime victim or the representatives of the crime victim's estate, family members, or any other persons appointed as suitable by the court, may assume the crime victim's rights under this chapter, but in no event shall the defendant be named as such guardian or representative.

(f) Procedures to promote compliance. —

(1) Regulations. — Not later than 1 year after the date of enactment of this chapter, the Attorney General of the United States shall promulgate regulations to enforce the rights of crime victims and to ensure compliance by responsible officials with the obligations described in law respecting crime victims.
(2) Contents. — The regulations promulgated under paragraph (1) shall —

(a) designate an administrative authority within the Department of Justice to receive and investigate complaints relating to the provision or violation of the rights of a crime victim;
(b) require a course of training for employees and offices of the Department of Justice that fail to comply with provisions of Federal law pertaining to the treatment of crime victims, and otherwise assist such employees and offices in responding more effectively to the needs of crime victims;
(c) contain disciplinary sanctions, including suspension or termination from employment, for employees of the Department of Justice who willfully or wantonly fail to comply with provisions of Federal law pertaining to the treatment of crime victims; and
(d) provide that the Attorney General, or the designee of the Attorney General, shall be the final arbiter of the complaint, and that there shall be no judicial review of the final decision of the Attorney General by a complainant.

Chapter 2

CRIME VICTIMS' RIGHTS ACT: A SKETCH OF 18 U.S.C. 3771*

SUMMARY

The victims of federal crimes enjoy certain rights to notice, attendance and participation in the federal criminal justice process by virtue of 18 U.S.C. 3771. More specifically, the section assures victims that they have:

> (1) The right to be reasonably protected from the accused. (2) The right to reasonable, accurate, and timely notice of any public court proceeding, or any parole proceeding, involving the crime or of any release or escape of the accused. (3) The right not to be excluded from any such public court proceeding, unless the court, after receiving clear and convincing evidence, determines that testimony by the victim would be materially altered if the victim heard other testimony at that proceeding. (4) The right to be reasonably heard at any public proceeding in the district court involving release, plea, sentencing, or any parole proceeding. (5) The reasonable right to confer with the attorney for the Government in the case. (6) The right to full and timely restitution as provided in law. (7) The right to proceedings free from unreasonable delay. (8) The right to be treated with fairness and with respect for the victim's dignity and privacy.

---

* Excerpted from CRS Report RS22518, Updated September 29, 2006

BACKGROUND

Section 3771 is the product of a decades-long effort to afford greater deference to victims in the criminal justice process. It is akin to the victims' bill of rights provisions found in the laws of the various states and augments a fairly wide variety of pre-existing federal victims' rights legislation. Its enactment followed closely on the heels of discontinued efforts to pass a victims' rights amendment to the United States Constitution.

WHO IS A VICTIM

The definition of "victim," the question of deciding who should be afforded rights and who should not be, was one of the difficulties that surfaced during the course of debates over the proposals to amend the United States Constitution. Section 3771 provides an explicit definition:

> For the purposes of this chapter, the term "crime victim" means a person directly and proximately harmed as a result of the commission of a Federal offense or an offense in the District of Columbia. In the case of a crime victim who is under 18 years of age, incompetent, incapacitated, or deceased, the legal guardians of the crime victim or the representatives of the crime victim's estate, family members, or any other persons appointed as suitable by the court, may assume the crime victim's rights under this chapter, but in no event shall the defendant be named as such guardian or representative. 18 U.S.C. 3771(e).

Other than the coverage of victims of crime under the laws of the District of Columbia, the definition is by and large the same definition found in the general federal restitution statutes, 18 U.S.C. 3663, 3663A. Commentators have suggested that courts will be able to draw upon the case law developed under the two restitution statutes to determine who qualifies as a victim under section 3771. Recourse may be somewhat complicated, however, by the presence of additional language in the restitution definitions, or by the references in the restitution statutes to specific persons and the types of harm that qualify for restitution. Nevertheless, the courts do seem likely to consult their experience under the restitution statutes when construing section 3771's definition of victim. Section 3771 and the restitution statutes speak of victims who are "persons" ("'crime victim" means a person . . ."). Although in common parlance, this might be thought to restrict the class of victims to human beings, general usage within the

United States Code is to the contrary. Unless the context suggests another intent, the word "person" as used in the United States Code is understood to "include corporations, companies, associations, firms, partnerships, societies, and joint stock companies as well as individuals," 1 U.S.C. 1. Some courts hold that restitution is only available for harm directly related to the crime of conviction or provided for in some explicit exception such as that available for conspiracies and plea bargains. Other courts will permit restitution based on proximate harm if it is not too remote from the crime of conviction and if there are no unrelated intervening causes or contributors to the harm. Thus for instance, a defendant convicted of bank robbery may be order to pay restitution for the damage he caused during his attempted getaway. Restitution is only available for harm related to the crime of conviction. Victims of crimes, other than those for which the defendant is convicted, are not entitled to restitution even if they were victims of offenses that were initially charged with the crime of conviction or are indisputably related to the crime of conviction. The same may hold true for victims under section 3771. Individuals may lose victim status under section 3771 during the course the criminal proceedings if charges covering the crimes of which they are the victim are dropped or dismissed even though related crimes continue to be prosecuted.

Like the restitution statutes, section 3771 states that in the case of a deceased victim, "the legal guardians of the crime victim or the representatives of the crime victim's estate, family members, or any other persons appointed as suitable by the court, *may assume the crime victim's rights*." This suggests that family members of the deceased are not as such considered victims without more. It implies that the parents and other relatives of an adult homicide victim may assume the victim's rights under the appointment of the court, but otherwise are entitled to none of section 3771's victims' benefits. The restitution cases may lend some credence to this view. Early case law construing section 3771 seems to leave the question unsettled.

THE RIGHT TO BE REASONABLY PROTECTED FROM THE ACCUSED

Section 3771 lists the right to be reasonably protected from the accused first among its victims rights. It appears to have been the subject of little, if any, judicial attention. One commentator has observed that "the legal significance, if any, of these general provisions is unclear." At the very least, the section provides an explicit justification for compatible judicial action taken in the interest of victim safety.

Notice

Section 3771's notification rights are subject to several limitations, some explicit, some implicit. The section explicitly excuses a failure to notify victims of the release of an accused when to do so might be dangerous, and it permits the courts to seek reasonable accommodations when the number of victims in a given case precludes strict compliance with the section's demands. The notice clause has several distinctive features: (1) the notice rights apply only with respect to *public court proceedings* and *parole proceedings*; (2) the rights attach to those proceedings *involving the crime* but not necessarily to all those related to the crime; (3) victims are entitled to *reasonable, accurate and timely* notice; and (4) victims are only entitled to notice of the release or escape of *the accused.* With regard to this last feature, committee reports on the equivalent language in the proposed constitutional amendment considered the terms "accused" and "convicted" interchangeable. The sponsors of section 3771 were of the same view.

Attendance

Section 3771 assures victims of the right not to be excluded from any public proceedings involving the crime except where to attend would color their subsequent testimony. It is one area where balancing the interests of victim, defendant, and government may be the most challenging.

Participation

Unlike the rights to notice and not to be excluded, the right to be heard is a right to participate. The section limits application to reasonable participation in public court and parole proceedings. It does not on its face give victims the right to be heard in closed proceedings or to be heard on other pre-trial motions, at trial, perhaps on appeal, or with respect to related forfeiture or habeas proceedings. Nor does it explicitly give the victim the right to be heard in any particular form.

Section 3771 assures crime victims of the right to reasonably be heard at proceedings where a plea bargain is accepted. The right only attaches to the acceptance of plea bargains in open court (i.e., at public proceedings). The right clearly does not vest a victim with the right to participate in plea negotiations between the defendant and the prosecutor, which are neither public nor proceedings. By the same token, the right to be heard is not the right to decide; victims must be heard, but their views are not necessarily controlling. It remains to be seen whether the existence of the right in open court will lead to more proceedings being closed to avoid the complications of recognizing the right.

The sponsors of the legislation seem to have anticipated that the right to heard at sentencing included the right to be heard orally and did not intend to permit the courts to require participation in writing except when faced with an overwhelming number of victims at the sentencing of single defendant. Thus far, the courts seem to concur.

Confer

The Senate sponsors said of the right to confer with the attorney for the government: This right is intended to be expansive. For example, the victim has the right to confer with the Government concerning any critical stage or disposition of the case.

This right to confer does not give the crime victim any right to direct the prosecution. Prosecutors should consider it part of their profession to be available to consult with crime victims about the concerns the victims may have which are pertinent to the case, case proceedings or dispositions. Under this provision, victims are able to confer with the Government's attorney about proceedings *after charging*. At least some courts appear to believe that exercise of the right must be self-initiated.

Restitution

The section affords the right to full and timely restitution as provided in law. It seems to confirm rather than enlarge existing law in the area of restitution. Sponsors felt that the rest of section would bolster the victim's restitution interest by ensuring the victim's rights to notice, consultation and participation. One appellate court has pointed out that the promise of "full" restitution extends only as far as the law provides, a fact that makes it clear that Congress recognized that there would be numerous situations when it would be impossible for multiple crime victims to the same set of crimes to be repaid every dollar they had lost.

Reasonable Freedom From Delay

Section 3771 continues to describe the right to delay avoidance in limiting terms. Its sponsors suggested than the right was aimed at scheduling delays. Early case law indicates that the courts are sensitive to victims' interest in delay avoidance, but also that in some instances delay may be in the interest of at least some victims.

Fairness, Dignity and Privacy

This right to be treated with fairness and respect for one's dignity and privacy rarely found explicit expression in the proposed constitutional amendments, although it clearly lies at the heart of all of them. The same language appears in the earlier federal "best efforts" statute, and a similar right is featured in many of the state constitutional and statutory victims' rights provisions.

Responsibilities of the Courts

At least one court has expressed the view that the provision in section 3771 designates the judiciary as an insurer of the rights of victims requires at least some proactive procedure designed to ensure victims' rights. The trial court's obligation to "ensure" victims' rights seems to set its responsibilities a notch above the "best efforts" level of obligation imposed upon other officials.

Responsibilities of Other Authorities

Section 3771 directs officers and employees of the Department of Justice and other departments and agencies of the United States engaged in the detection, investigation, or prosecution of crime to make their best efforts to see that crime victims are notified of, and accorded, the rights the section confers. It specifically instructs prosecutors to advise crime victims that they can seek the advice of an attorney with respect to those rights.

ENFORCEMENT

Section 3771 expressly authorizes the government to assert rights on behalf of the victim. The government's prerogative to assert the rights of a victim apparently includes the right to petition for mandamus when they are denied. Victims also enjoy a right to appeal denial of any their statutory rights using a writ of mandamus. At least two federal appellate courts have concluded that since Congress had designated mandamus as the principal avenue of review, it did not intend to require victims to overcome the hurdles typically faced by petitioner seek review of a district court determination through a writ of mandamus.

NO NEW RIGHTS FOR THE ACCUSED

A person accused of the crime may not obtain any form of relief under section 3771, nor may denial of a right under the section provide grounds for a new trial.

MANY VICTIMS — ONE ACCUSED

In a case where the court finds that the number of crime victims makes it impracticable to accord all of the crime victims the rights described in the section, the court shall fashion a reasonable procedure to give effect to the section that does not unduly complicate or prolong the proceedings.

NO DAMAGES

The constitutional amendment proposals generally included a ban on damages. They were thought to not only to bar a cause of action for damages on behalf of aggrieved victims but also to preclude requests for the appointment of counsel to represent indigent victims or for payment of attorneys fees for retained counsel. The sponsors of section 3771 made no similar statements during the course of debate with respect to the damage ban found in section 3771, but did point out that other sections of the legislation established a grant program to provide victims with legal assistance. Other Members bemoaned the fact that the section makes no provision for the appointment of counsel for indigent victims.

JUSTICE DEPARTMENT REGULATIONS

The Attorney General's regulations required by section 3771 must include the designation of an official to receive victim complaints concerning performance under the section, training for Justice Department employees, and disciplinary sanctions for willful and wanton violations, 18 U.S.C. 3771(f)(2). The Department of Justice issued revised victim assistance guidelines in May 2005 that include section 3771 matters, United States Department of Justice, Office of Justice Programs, Office of Victims of Crime, *Attorney General Guidelines for Victim and Witness Assistance* (May 2005), available on September 27, 2006 at, [http://www.usdoj.gov/olp/final.pdf].

REFERENCES

[1] Section 3771 was enacted as part of the Scott Campbell, Stephanie Roper, Wendy Preston, Louarna Gillis, and Nila Lynn Crime Victims' Rights Act (CVRA), which in turn appears as Title I of the Justice For All Act of 2004, P.L. 108-405, 118 Stat. 2260 (2004). The text of section 3771 is appended.

[2] *But What about the Victim? The Forsaken Man in American Criminal Law*, 22 UNIVERSITY OF FLORIDA LAW REVIEW 1, 10-20 (1969)(describing early state victim compensation statutes); The President's Commission on Law Enforcement and Administration of Justice, Task Force on Assessment, *Task Force Report: Crimes and Its Impact — An Assessment* 83 (1967)("The Commission has been impressed by the consensus among legislators and law enforcement officials that some kind of State compensation for victims of violent crime is desirable").

[3] Tanford & Bocchino, *Rape Victim Shield Laws and the Sixth Amendment*, 128 UNIVERSITY OF PENNSYLVANIA LAW REVIEW 544, 544, 550 n.23 (1979)("In the past few years, forty-six states have made efforts to protect rape victims from the humiliation of public disclosure of the details of their prior sexual activities")(also noting the elimination of corroboration requirements that refused to allow a rape conviction based solely upon the testimony of the victim); see also, Berger, *Man's Trial, Woman's Tribulation: Rape Cases in the Courtroom*, 77 COLUMBIA LAW REVIEW 1 (1977).

[4] *Highway Safety — Menace on Our Highways — Is Implied Consent the Answer?* 18 DEPAUL LAW REVIEW 753, 754 n.7 (1969)(noting

the trend to enact implied consent to statutes to permit authorities to test the blood alcohol level of suspected drunken drivers).

[5] *Bail Reform in the State and Federal Systems*, 20 VANDERBILT LAW REVIEW 948, 959-60 (1967)(noting the preventive detention tendency of state courts to consider, in setting bail, the danger of the accused to the community including past and future victims); see also Mitchell, *Bail Reform and the Constitutionality of Pretrial Detention*, 55 VIRGINIA LAW REVIEW 1223, 1236 (1969)(noting that the Administration's preventive detention proposals were limited to crimes which usually "involve planning, deliberation and the purposeful selection of a victim who is almost always a stranger").

[6] Talbert, *The Relevance of Victim Impact Statements to the Criminal Sentencing Decision*, 36 UCLA LAW REVIEW 199, 200-201 & n.12 (1988)(noting that by the mid-1980's at least thirty-eight states had enacted statutes calling for some form of victim impact statement at sentencing).

[7] Ala.Const., Amend. 557; Alaska Const. Art.I, §24; Ariz.Const. Art.2, §2.1; Cal. Const. Art.I, §28; Colo.Const. Art.Ii, §16a; Conn.Const. Art.I, §8[B.]; Fla.Const. Art.I, §16(B); Idaho Const. Art.I, §22; Ill.Const. Art.I, §8.1; Ind.Const. Art.1, §13; La.Const. Art.1, §25; Kan.Const. Art.15, §15; Md.D.Of Rts. Art.47; Mich.Const. Art.I, §24; Miss. Const. Art. 3,§26a; Mo.Const. Art.I, §32; Mont. Const. Art.2, §28; Neb.Const. Art.1, §28; Nev.Const. Art.1, §8; N.J. Const. Art.I, §22; N.Mex. Const. Art.Ii, §24; N.C.Const. Art.I, §37; Ohio Const. Art.I, §10a; Okla.Const. Art.Ii, §34; Ore.Const. Art. I, §24; R.I. Const. Art.I, §23; S.C.Const. Art.I, §24; Tenn.Const. Art.I, §35; Tex.Const. Art.I, §30; Utah Const. Art.I, §28; Va.Const. Art.I, §8-A; Wash.Const. Art.I, §35; Wis. Const. Art.I, §9m.

[8] Ala.Code §§15-23-60 To 15-23-84; Alaska Stat. §§12.61.010 To 12.61.050; Ariz.Rev. Stat.Ann. §§13-4401 To 13-4438; Ark.Code Ann. §§16-90-1101 To 16-90-1115; Cal. Penal Code §§679 To 679.04; Colo.Rev.Stat.Ann. §§24-4.1-301 To 24-4.1-304; Conn. Gen.Stat.Ann. §§54-201 To 54-233; Del.Code Ann. Tit.11 §§9401 To 9419; Fla.Stat. Ann. §§960.001 To 960.297; Ga.Code Ann. §§ 17-17-1 To 17-17-165; Haw.Rev.Stat. §§801d-1 To 801d-7; Idaho Code §19-5306; Ill.Comp.Laws Ann. Ch.725 §§120/1 To 120/9; Ind.Code Ann. §§35-40-5-1 To 35-40-5-9; Iowa Code Ann. §§915.1 To 915.100; Kan.Stat.Ann. §74-7333; Ky.Rev.Stat.Ann. §§421.500 To 421.550; La.Rev.Stat.Ann. §§46:1841 To 46:1844; Me.Rev.Stat.Ann. Tit.17-A §§1171 To 1175; Md.Code Ann. Art.27 §§761 To 789; Mass.Gen.Laws Ann. Ch.258b

§§1 To 13; Mich.Comp.Laws Ann. §§780.751 To 780.834; Minn.Stat.Ann. §§611a.01 To 611a.90; Miss.Code Ann. §§99- 43-1 To 99-43-49; Mo.Ann.Stat. §§595.200 To 595.218; Mont.Code Ann. §§46-24-101 To 46-24-213; Neb.Rev.Stat. §81-1848; Nev.Rev.Stat. §§178.569 To 178.571; N.H.Rev. Stat.Ann. §21-M:8-K; N.J.Stat.Ann. §§52:4b-36 To 52:4b-49; N.Mex.Stat.Ann. §§31- 26-1 To 31-26-14; N.Y.Exec.Law §§640 To 649; N.C.Gen.Stat. §§15a-830 To 15a-841; N.D.Cent.Code §§12.1-34-01 To 12.1-34-05; Ohio Rev.Code Ann. §§2930.01 To 2930.19; Okla.Stat.Ann. Tit. 19 §215.33; Ore.Rev.Stat. §§147.405 To 147.421; Pa.Stat.Ann. Tit.18 §11.201; R.I.Gen.Laws §§12-28-1 To 12-28-12; S.C.Code Ann. §§16-3-1510 To 16-3- 1565; S.D.Cod.Laws Ann. §§23a-28c-1 To 23a-28c-6; Tenn.Code Ann. §§40-38-101 To 40-38-108; Tex.Code Of Crim.Pro. Arts.56.01 To 56.12; Utah Code Ann. §§77-38-1 To 77-38-14; Vt.Stat.Ann. Tit.13 §§5301 To 5321; Va.Code Ann. §§19.2-11.01 To 19.2-11.4; Wash.Rev.Code Ann. §§7.69.020 To 7.69.030; W.Va.Code §§61-11a-1 To 61-11a-8; Wis.Stat.Ann. §§950.01 To 950.11; Wyo.Stat. §§1-40-201 To 1-40-210.

[9] *E.g.*, 18 U.S.C. 3510 (victim attendance rights), 3525 (victims compensation fund), 3555 (notice to fraud victims), 3663-3664 (restitution), F.R.Crim.P. 32(i)(4)(B)(victim impact statements at sentencing), F.R.Evid. 412 (relevancy of victims' past conduct).

[10] Congress repealed section 10606 when it enacted section 3771, P.L. 108-405, §102(c), 118 Stat. 2264 (2004).

[11] 104 Stat. 4822 (1990), 42 U.S.C. 10606 nt ("It is the sense of Congress that the States should make every effort to adopt the following goals of the Victims of Crime Bill of Rights: (1) Victims of crime should be treated with compassion, respect and dignity throughout the criminal justice process. (2) Victims of crime should be reasonably protected from the accused throughout the criminal justice process. (3) Victims of crime should have a statutorily designated advisory role in decisions involving prosecutorial discretion, such as the decision to plea-bargain. (4) Victims of crime should have the right to a reasonable assurance that the accused will be tried in an expeditious manner. (5) A victim of crime should have the right to be present at all proceedings related to the offense against him, unless the victim is to testify and the court determines that the victim's testimony would be materially prejudiced by hearing other testimony at the trial. (6) Victims of crime should have the right to information about the conviction, sentencing and imprisonment of the person who

committed the crime against them. (7) Victims of crime should be compensated for the damage resulting from the crime to the fullest extent possible by the person convicted of the crime. (8) Victims of crime should have a statutorily designated advisory role in deciding the early release status of the person convicted of the crime against them. (9) A victim of crime should never be forced to endure again the emotional and physical consequences of the original crime").

[12] 42 U.S.C. 10607(a)("*Designation of responsible officials*. The head of each department and agency of the United States engaged in the detection, investigation, or prosecution of crime shall designate by names and office titles the persons who will be responsible for identifying the victims of crime and performing the services described in subsection (c) of this section at each stage of a criminal case. "(b) *Identification of victims*. At the earliest opportunity after the detection of a crime at which it may be done without interfering with an investigation, a responsible official shall — (1) identify the victim or victims of a crime; (2) inform the victims of their right to receive, on request, the services described in subsection (c) of this section; and (3) inform each victim of the name, title, and business address and telephone number of the responsible official to whom the victim should address a request for each of the services described in subsection (c) of this section. "(c) *Description of services*. (1) A responsible official shall — (A) inform a victim of the place where the victim may receive emergency medical and social services; (B) inform a victim of any restitution or other relief to which the victim may be entitled under this or any other law and manner in which such relief may be obtained; (C) inform a victim of public and private programs that are available to provide counseling, treatment, and other support to the victim; and (D) assist a victim in contacting the persons who are responsible for providing the services and relief described in subparagraphs (A), (B), and (C). (2) A responsible official shall arrange for a victim to receive reasonable protection from a suspected offender and persons acting in concert with or at the behest of the suspected offender. (3) During the investigation and prosecution of a crime, a responsible official shall provide a victim the earliest possible notice of — (A) the status of the investigation of the crime, to the extent it is appropriate to inform the victim and to the extent that it will not interfere with the investigation; (B) the arrest of a suspected offender; (C) the filing of charges against a suspected offender; (D) the scheduling of each court proceeding that the witness is either

required to attend or, under section 10606(b)(4) of this title, is entitled to attend; (E) the release or detention status of an offender or suspected offender; (F) the acceptance of a plea of guilty or nolo contendere or the rendering of a verdict after trial; and (G) the sentence imposed on an offender, including the date on which the offender will be eligible for parole. (4) During court proceedings, a responsible official shall ensure that a victim is provided a waiting area removed from and out of the sight and hearing of the defendant and defense witnesses. (5) After trial, a responsible official shall provide a victim the earliest possible notice of — (A) the scheduling of a parole hearing for the offender; (B) the escape, work release, furlough, or any other form of release from custody of the offender; and (C) the death of the offender, if the offender dies while in custody. (6) At all times, a responsible official shall ensure that any property of a victim that is being held for evidentiary purposes be maintained in good condition and returned to the victim as soon as it is no longer needed for evidentiary purposes. (7) The Attorney General or the head of another department or agency that conducts an investigation of a sexual assault shall pay, either directly or by reimbursement of payment by the victim, the cost of a physical examination of the victim which an investigating officer determines was necessary or useful for evidentiary purposes. The Attorney General shall provide for the payment of the cost of up to 2 anonymous and confidential tests of the victim for sexually transmitted diseases, including HIV, gonorrhea, herpes, Chlamydia, and syphilis, during the 12 months following sexual assaults that pose a risk of transmission, and the cost of a counseling session by a medically trained professional on the accuracy of such tests and the risk of transmission of sexually transmitted diseases to the victim as the result of the assault. A victim may waive anonymity and confidentiality of any tests paid for under this section. (8) A responsible official shall provide the victim with general information regarding the corrections process, including information about work release, furlough, probation, and eligibility for each. "(d) *No cause of action or defense*. This section does not create a cause of action or defense in favor of any person arising out of the failure of a responsible person to provide information as required by subsection (b) or (c) of this section. "(e) *Definitions*. For the purposes of this section — (1) the term "responsible official" means a person designated pursuant to subsection (a) of this section to perform the functions of a responsible official under that section; and (2) the term "victim" means a person that has suffered direct physical, emotional, or pecuniary harm as a result of the commission of a crime, including — (A) in the case of a victim that is an institutional entity, an authorized representative of the entity; and (B) in the case of a victim who is under 18 years of age, incompetent, incapacitated, or deceased, one of the following (in order of preference): (i) a spouse; (ii) a legal guardian; (iii) a parent; (iv) a child; (v) a sibling; (vi) another family member; or (vii) another person designated by the court").

[13] *See,* in the 104th Congress: S.J.Res. 52, S.J.Res. 65, H.J.Res. 173, and H.J.Res. 174; *A Proposed Constitutional Amendment to Establish a Bill of Rights for Crime Victims: Hearing Before the Senate Comm. on the Judiciary*, 104th Cong., 2d Sess. (1996) — in 105th Congress: S.J.Res. 6, S.J.Res. 44, H.J.Res. 71, and H.J.Res. 129; S.Rept. 105-409 (1998); *Proposals to Provide Rights to Victims of Crime: Hearing Before the House Comm. on the Judiciary*, 105th Cong., 1st Sess. (1997); *A Proposed Constitutional Amendment to Protect Victims of Crime: Hearing Before the Senate Comm. on the Judiciary*, 105th Cong., 1st Sess. (1997) — in the 106th Congress: S.J.Res. 3, and H.J.Res. 64; S.Rept. 106-254 (2000); *A Proposed Constitutional Amendment to Protect Crime Victims: Hearing Before the Senate Comm. on the Judiciary*, 106th Cong., 1st Sess. (1999), and *H.J.Res. 64, Proposing An Amendment to the Constitution of the United States to Protect the Rights of Crime Victims: Hearing Before the Subcommittee on the Constitution of the House Judiciary Comm.*, 106th Cong., 2d Sess. (2000); — in the 107th Congress: S.J.Res. 35, H.J.Res. 88, and H.J.Res. 91; *Federal Victims Rights Amendment: Hearing Before the Subcomm. on the Constitution of the House Comm. on the Judiciary*, 107th Cong., 2d Sess. (2002)(*House Hearing IV*); *S.J.Res.35-The Crime Victims' Rights Amendment: Hearing Before the Subcomm. on Constitution, Federalism, and Property Rights of the Senate Comm. on the Judiciary*, 107th Cong., 2d Sess. (2002)(*Senate Hearing IV*); and — in the 108th Congress: H.J.Res. 10, H.J.Res. 48, S.J.Res.1; S.Rept. 108-191; *Crime Victims Constitutional Amendment: Hearing Before the Subcomm. on the Constitution of the House Comm. on the Judiciary* , 108th Cong., 1st Sess. (2003)(*House Hearing V*); *A Proposed Constitutional Amendment to Protect Crime Victims, S.J.Res.1: Hearing Before the Senate Comm. on the Judiciary*; 108th Cong., 1st Sess. (2003)*(Senate Hearing V).*

[14] "[R]ecognizing that we didn't have the 67 votes necessary for a constitutional amendment — both Senator Kyl and I, as well as the

victims and their advocates, decided that we should compromise. There are Members of this body who very much want a statute. There are Members of this body who very much want a constitutional amendment. We have drafted a statute which we believe is broad and encompassing. . . ." 150 *Cong.Rec.* S4261 (daily ed. April 22, 2004)(remarks of Sen. Feinstein); *see also*, *Id.* at S4266 ("Knowing we would not have the 67 votes to pass it, we decided it was time to get something tangible in statute to protect the rights of victims")(remarks of Sen. Kyl).

[15] 150 *Cong. Rec.* S4279 (daily ed. April 22, 2004).

[16] 150 *Cong. Rec.* H8208-209 (daily ed. Oct. 6, 2004). See also, H.Rept. 108-711(2004).

[17] 150 *Cong. Rec.* S10910 (daily ed. Oct. 9, 2004).

[18] P.L. 108-405, 118 Stat. 2260 (2004).

[19] *Cf.*, S.Rept. 105-409 (additional views of Sen. Hatch); Barnard, *Allocution for Victims of Economic Crimes*, 77 NOTRE DAME LAW REVIEW 39 (2001).

[20] *United States v. Degenhardt*, 405 F.Supp.2d 1341, 1342-345 (D. Utah 2005). Past proposed constitutional amendments sometimes referred to the victims of felonies, *e.g.*, H.J.Res. 64 (105th Cong.), H.J.Res. 173 (104th Cong.). The fact that section 3771 simply refers to "crime" indicates that the section is intended to apply to the victim of any federal crime, regardless of its classification. The issue of whether misconduct that is punishable only with a monetary sanction should be considered a crime for purposes of section 3771 may be more problematic.

[21] *E.g.*, Cassell, *Recognizing Victims in the Federal Rules of Criminal Procedure: Proposed Amendments in Light of the Crime Victims' Rights Act*, 2005 BRIGHAM YOUNG UNIVERSITY LAW REVIEW 835, 857.

[22] "For the purposes of this chapter, the term 'crime victim' means a person directly and proximately harmed as a result of the commission of an offense *for which restitution may be ordered including, in the case of an offense that involves an element of a scheme, conspiracy, or pattern of criminal activity, any person directly harmed by the defendant's criminal conduct in the course of the scheme, conspiracy, or pattern.* In the case of a crime victim who is under 18 years of age, incompetent, incapacitated, or deceased, the legal guardians of the crime victim or the representatives of the crime victim's estate, family members, or any other persons appointed as suitable by the court, may

assume the crime victim's rights under this chapter, but in no event shall the defendant be named as such guardian or representative," 18 U.S.C. 3663(a)(2), 3663A(a)(2)(language that does not appear in section 3771 in italics).

[23] "If a victim has received compensation from insurance or any other source with respect to a loss, the court shall order that restitution be paid to the person who provided or is obligated to provide the compensation, but the restitution order shall provide that all restitution of victims required by the order be paid to the victims before any restitution is paid to such a provider of compensation," 18 U.S.C. 3664(j)(1). " . . . [W]hen sentencing a defendant convicted of an offense described in [various] section[s] . . . of the Controlled Substances Act . . . the court may order that the defendant make restitution in accordance with this subsection. . . . (3) Restitution under this subsection shall be distributed as follows: (A) 65 percent of the total amount of restitution shall be paid to the State entity designated to administer crime victim assistance in the State in which the crime occurred. (B) 35 percent of the total amount of restitution shall be paid to the State entity designated to receive Federal substance abuse block grant funds," 18 U.S.C. 3663(c)(1), (3).

[24] "The order of restitution shall require that such defendant . . . (2) in the case of an offense resulting in bodily injury to a victim — (A) pay an amount equal to the cost of necessary medical and related professional services and devices relating to physical, psychiatric, and psychological care, including nonmedical care and treatment rendered in accordance with a method of healing recognized by the law of the place of treatment," 18 U.S.C. 3663A(b)(2)(A); *United States v. Reichow*, 416 F.3d 802, 805 (8th Cir. 2005)(holding that in the absence of a bodily injury, a bank robber could not be ordered to pay restitution to cover the costs of psychiatric counseling for the bank's tellers).

[25] *United States v. Streebing*, 987 F.2d 368, (6th Cir. 1993); *United States v. Kirkland*, 853 F.2d 1243, 1246 (5th Cir. 1988); *United States v. Sunrhodes*, 831 F.2d 1537, 1545-546 (10th Cir. 1987); *United States v. Ruffen*, 780 F.2d 1493, 1496 (9th Cir. 1986).

[26] *See e.g., United States v. Davenport*, 445 F.3d 366, 374 (4th Cir. 2006)(credit card company); *United States v. Washington*, 434 F.3d 1265, 1268-270 (11th Cir. 2006) (condominium association).

[27] *United States v. Ekanem*, 383 F.3d 40, 42-3 (2d Cir. 2004)("But the meaning of 'victim' under MVRA [the Mandatory Victims Restitution

Act, 18 U.S.C. 3663A], contrary to defendant's position is not controlled by the default definition of 'person' in the Dictionary Act — which excludes the Government — because that definition does not apply if the 'context [of a particular statute] indicates otherwise,' 1 U.S.C. 1. . . .[W]e conclude that the context of MVRA indicates otherwise, so that the term 'victim' as used in that statute is not limited by the default definition of 'person' in the Dictionary Act but instead includes the Government"); *see also*, *United States v. Washington*, 434 F.3d 1265, 1268-270 (11th Cir. 2006)(upholding a restitution order in favor a police department whose vehicles a bank robber damaged in his attempted getaway); *United States v. Phillips*, 367 F.3d 846, (9th Cir. 2004)(Environmental Protection Agency may be the qualified beneficiary of a restitution order); *United States v. Caldwell*, 302 F.3d 399, 419-20 (5th Cir. 2002)(State of Mississippi may entitled to an award of restitution). Nevertheless, while an government may be victimized, the courts will ordinarily not order restitution to cover the government's costs in the operation of a sting or other costs associated with the investigation and prosecution of the defendant, *United States v. Phillips*, 367 F.3d 846, 863 (9th Cir. 2004); *United States v. Cottman*, 142 F.3d 160, 168-69 (3d Cir. 1998); *United States v. Khawaja*, 118 F.3d 1454, 1460 (11th Cir. 1997); *United States v. Meacham*, 27 F.3d 214, 218-19 (6th Cir. 1994); *United States v. Daddato*, 996 F.2d 903, 905 (7th Cir. 1993); *United States v. Salcedo-Lopez*, 907 F.2d 97, 98 (9th Cir. 1990).

[28] *E.g.*, *United States v. Davenport*, 445 F.3d 366, 374 (4th Cir. 2006)("A person is directly harmed for purposes of MVRA when the harm results form conduct underlying an element of the offense of conviction and adding term proximately does not broaden the definition of victim"); *United States v. Donaby*, 349 F.3d 1046, 1052 (7th Cir. 2003)(There are "three situations in which restitution is authorized under MVRA: (1) to a victim directly harmed by the offender's specific conduct that is the basis for the offense of conviction, (2) to a victim who is directly harmed by the offender's conduct in course of committing an offense that involves s an element a scheme, conspiracy or pattern, or (3) if the parties so agreed in a plea bargain").

[29] *United States v. LaFuente,* 353 F.3d 766, 772 (9th Cir. 2003) (upholding restitution order for the benefit of the Postal Service, the fire department's hazardous materials division, and the county health department for the costs of the remedial actions they took in response

to the defendant's mailing letters containing powder purporting to be anthrax)("The main inquiry for causation in investigation cases is whether there was an intervening cause, and if so, whether this intervening cause was directly related to the offense. [The] Defendant's conduct need not be the sole cause of the loss, but any subsequent action that contributes to the loss such as an intervening cause must be directly related to the defendant's conduct. We have approved restitution awards that included losses at least one step removed from the offense conduct itself, but the causal chain may not extend so far, in terms of the facts or the time span, as to become unreasonable")(internal citations and quotation marks omitted). *See also*, *United States v. Gamma Tech Industries, Inc.*, 265 F.3d 917, 927-28 (9th Cir. 2001)("In several cases, we have concluded that losses did not result directly from a defendant's criminal conduct, because either there was an unrelated, intervening cause, or the criminal conduct to which a defendant pleaded guilty did not cause the loss. *See e.g., United States v. Meksian,* 170 F.3d 1260, 1263 (9th Cir. 1999)(rejecting mere 'but for' standard for proving loss and reversing restitution order in fraudulent loan application case because an intervening cause for the erroneous issuance of the loan, an inaccurate environment report, was not directly related to the offense conduct); *United States v. Sablan*, 92 F.3d 865, 870 (9th Cir. 1996) (reversing restitution order based on consequential damages, such as expenses arising from meetings with law enforcement officers investigating the crime, because such expenses were not necessary to repair damage caused by defendant's criminal conduct); *United States v. Reed*, 80 F.3d 1419, 1421 (9th Cir. 1996)(reversing restitution order based on damage to private vehicles occurring during flight form police where the offense of conviction was illegal possession of a firearm by a felon); *United States v. Tyler*, 767 F.2 1350, 1351 (9th Cir. 1985)(rejecting restitution awarded under then 3651 because losses based on depressed market prices were too remote). "However, we have approved restitution awards that included losses at least one step removed from the offense conduct itself. *See e.g., United States v. Rice*, 38 F.3d 1536, 1542 (9th Cir. 1994)(upholding in conspiracy and mail fraud case, restitution based n victim's inability to use entire inventory of parts supplied by defendant because victim could not identify which parts were defective); [*United States v.*] *Koenig*, 952 F.2d [267], 274-75 [(9th Cir. 1991)(upholding, in case involving conspiracy to produce and use counterfeit automated teller machine cards, restitution for the cost of reprogramming bank computers after defendants had stolen ATM account information).

[30] *United States v. Washington*, 434 F.3d 1265, 1269 (11th Cir. 2006)(emphasis of the court) ("The appropriate standard of causation is found in the restitution act itself: directly and proximately harmed *as a result of* the commission of an offense for which restitution may be ordered. Because the district court found Washington's flight was causally related to the bank robbery . . . we affirm restitution"); *accord United States v. Reichow*, 416 F.3d 802, 805 (8th Cir. 2005); *United States v. Donaby*, 349 F.3d 1046, 1053 (7th Cir. 2003).

[31] *United States v. Rand*, 403 F.3d 489, 493 (7th Cir. 2005)(identity thief could only be required to make restitution to those victims covered by his plea agreement); *United States v. Randle*, 324 F.3d 550 (7th Cir. 2003)(defendant charged with defrauding three victims could only be ordered to pay restitution to the victims covered by his plea agreement); *United States v. Elias*, 269 F.3d 1003, 1021-22(9th Cir. 2001)(defendant convicted a making a false statement concerning his handling of hazardous waste could not be ordered to pay restitution to a victim harmed by exposure to the waste); *cf., United States v. Inman*, 411 F.3d 591, 595 (5th Cir. 2005)(defendant convicted fraudulent use of his employer's credit card could not be ordered to make restitution for credit card charges incurred prior to the time covered by his indictment and conviction).

[32] *United States v. Dayea*, 73 F.3d 229, 232 (9th Cir. 1995) (wife of a manslaughter victim was not entitled to restitution for her husband's lost income because *she* was not physically injured). Restitution statute authorizes awards for victims who suffered physical injuries and those who suffer damage to or loss of property, 18 U.S.C. 3663. Had the court considered the widow a victim in her husband's killing she would presumably have been eligible for restitution for lost income, *cf., United States v. Fountain*, 768 F.2d 792, 801 (7th Cir. 1985)(restitution order for the lost wages to the estate of homicide victim is proper); *United States v. Serawop*, 409 F.Supp.2d 1356, (D. Utah 2006)(same).

[33] *See also, United States v. Marcello*, 370 F.Supp.2d 745, (N.D.Ill. 2005)(declining a motion to permit the son of a homicide victim to make an oral statement (rather than a written statement) at sentencing but treating without discussion the motion as that of a victim); *United States v. Hairson*, 888 F.2d 1349, 1355 (11th Cir. 1989)(noting, in dicta with regard the restitution statute prior to the amendment that

limited the restitution to direct and proximate harm, that in the legislative history the Senate Report, S.Rept. 97-532 at 13 (1982), "states that . . . the definition of 'victims' is purposely broad to include indirect victims, such as family members of victims").

[34] "If a victim is under 18 years of age, incompetent, incapacitated, or deceased, a family member or legal guardian of the victim, a representative of the victim's estate, or any other person so appointed by the court may exercise the victim's rights. . ." United States Department of Justice, Office of Justice Programs, Office of Victims of Crime, *Attorney General Guidelines for Victim and Witness Assistance*, 9 (May 2005), available on September 27, 2006 at, [http://www.usdoj.gov/olp/final.pdf].

[35] *E.g.,* S.J.Res.3 (106th Cong.)("The rights and immunities established by this article shall apply in Federal and State proceedings, including military proceedings to the extent that the Congress may provide by law, juvenile justice proceedings, and proceedings in the District of Columbia and any commonwealth, territory, or possession of the United States"); H.J.Res. 64 (106th Cong.)(same).

[36] Some may consider the inclusion of the District of Columbia something of a curiosity since the D.C. Code already featured extensive crime victims' rights provisions, D.C. CODE §§23-1901 to 23-1906. Victims would appear to be free to claim the rights afforded by either section 3771 or the D.C. Code provisions.

[37] *E.g.*, Guam Code Ann. tit. §§160.10 et seq.; P.R. Laws Ann. tit. 25 §§973 et seq.; V.I. Code Ann. tit. 34 §§201 et seq.

[38] The point may be largely academic since Defense Department Directive 1030.1 (April 13, 2004) is a rough equivalent of subsection 3771(a).

[39] *United States v. L.M.*, 425 F.Supp.2d 948, 957 (N.D. Iowa 2006)(denying the motion of the family of a deceased minor victim to attend the hearing held to determine whether to transfer the juvenile for trial as an adult based on the court's decision to close the proceedings to the public).

[40] S.J.Res. 1 (108th Cong.) ("the right to adjudicative decisions that duly consider the victim's safety"); H.J.Res. 48 (108th Cong.).

[41] 150 *Cong. Rec.* S4267 (daily ed. April 22, 2004)(remarks of Sen. Feinstein)("I would like to turn to the bill itself and address the first section (a)(1), the right of the crime victim to be reasonably protected. Of course, the Government cannot protect the crime victim in all circumstances. However, where reasonable, the crime victim should

be provided accommodations such as a secure waiting area, away from the defendant before and after and during breaks in the proceedings").

[42] 150 *Cong.Rec.* S4270 (daily ed. April 22, 2004)(remarks of Sens. Feinstein and Kyl) ("One final point. Throughout this act, reference is made to the 'accused.' Would the Senator also agree that it is our intention to use this word in the broadest sense to include both those charged and convicted so that the rights we establish apply throughout the criminal justice system? "Mr. KLY. Yes, that []is my understanding").

[43] 150 *Cong.Rec.* S4267 (daily ed. April 22, 2004)(remarks of Sen. Feinstein), quoted *supra* n. 41.

[44] Beloof, VICTIMS IN CRIMINAL PROCEDURE 93 (1999).

[45] *See e.g.*, Cassell, *Recognizing Victims in the Federal Rules of Criminal Procedure: Proposed Amendments in Light of the Crime Victims' Rights Act*, 2005 BRIGHAM YOUNG UNIVERSITY LAW REVIEW 835, 874-73 (recommending a change in the Federal Rules of Criminal Procedure, that entitle a defendant to the identity of witnesses against him, to require a showing of special need before providing defendants with a victim's address and phone number); *but consider*, *United States v. Turner*, 367 F.Supp.2d 319, 332(E.D.N.Y. 2005)("*The right to be reasonably protected from the accused.*' 18 U.S.C. 3771(a)(1). Regardless of what this right might entail outside the bail context, it appears to add no new substance to the protection of crime victims afforded by the Bail Reform Act, which already allows a court to order reasonable conditions of release or the detention of an accused defendant to 'assure . . . the safety of any other person.' 18 U.S.C. 3142(c)(1). Other participatory rights in the CVRA give the victim standing to be heard independent of any presentation the prosecutor might make, but those rights do not appear to change the substantive bases on which a defendant can be released or detained").

[46] 150 *Cong. Rec.* S4267-268 (daily ed. April 22, 2004)(remarks of Sens. Kyl and Feinstein). Notice also allows victims to evaluate whether to begin civil proceedings against those associated with an offense but who may not have been prosecuted, *see e.g.*, *United States v. Crompton Corp.*, 399 F.Supp.2d 1047, 1051("Defendant requests redaction of [Defendant's CEO] Calarco's name because it wants to shield his identity from civil plaintiffs that have sued Defendant in dozens of lawsuits across the country . . . . [R]edacting Calarco's name wold violate the Crime Victims' Rights Act. Here, the plaintiffs in the additional civil lawsuits filed against Defendant are those who were

directly and proximately harmed as a result of the commission the antitrust violation. Therefore, the Court should be particularly sensitive to ensuring they are given full access to the proceedings and the Plea Agreement. Accordingly, the Court finds that redacting Calcarco's name from the Plea Agreement would violate the Crime Victims' Rights Act") (N.D.Cal. 2005).

[47] 18 U.S.C. 3771(c)(3).

[48] 18 U.S.C. 3771(d)(2).

[49] *United States v. Grace*, 401 F.Supp. 1057, 1063-64 (D.Mont. 2005)("Most of the statements made by the [Justice Department Victim Witness] Specialist are probably within the 'legitimate law enforcement purpose' exception [of the local rule barring pre-trial publicity] because there were made in the course of fulfilling of DOJ's duties under the Justice For All Act. This is so even if the statements should not have been made in the manner they were. Although these statements were made in public and disseminated in at least one local newspaper, they relate to topics that the DOJ is arguably required to address under the Justice For All Act, including a right to have timely notice of proceedings"). The court subsequently denied the defendant's motion for a change of venue predicated upon prejudicial pretrial publicity, *United States v. Grace*, 408 F.Supp. 998 (D.Mont. 2005). In doing so, it found it unnecessary to consider the government's argument that the interests of the victim community should be counted against the motion because the court did not "believe community interests warrant separate consideration beyond the Ninth Circuit's presumption against transfer of venue based on presumed prejudice," 408 F.Supp. at 1020-21.

[50] 18 U.S.C. 3771(c)(1).

[51] *E.g.*, S.J.Res. 65 (104th Cong.); H.J.Res. 71 (105th Cong.); S.J.Res. 3 (106th Cong.).

[52] *E.g.*, ARIZ.CONST. art. 2, §2.1(12); IND.CODE ANN. §35-40-5-9; LA.CONST. art.1, §25; MD.DECL.OF RTS. art.47(b); MASS.GEN.LAWS ANN. ch.258B, §3; N.J.STAT.ANN. §52:4B-42; ORE.CONST. art.I, §42; TENN.COST. art.I, §35; WYO.STAT. §1-40-203.

[53] "Victims' rights are of little use if victims remain unaware of them. Since victims deserve the eight basic rights [of the amendment], they should be informed about those rights. Not only does this serve to ensure that victims can exercise their rights, but it can even improve the functioning fo the criminal justice process. Victims who have

been informed about their role in the process are in a better position to cooperate with police, prosecutors, and courts to bring about a proper resolution of the case. Victims deserve appropriate notice of their rights in the process," S.Rept. 106-254 at 26.

[54] "I have significant concerns about the necessity and wisdom of . . . providing that covered victims shall have right 'to reasonable notice of the rights established' by the amendment. No other constitutional provision mandates that citizens be provided notice of the rights vested by the Constitution — not even the court-created *Miranda* warnings are constitutionally required. In an analogous context, Justice O'Connor noted that 'the free exercise clause is written in terms of what the Government cannot do to the individual, not in terms of what the individual can exact from the Government,' This clause in the proposed victims' rights amendment would create an affirmative duty on the Government to provide notice of what rights the Constitution provides, turning this formulation on its head. "Moreover, I do not believe that sufficient consideration has been given to the practical aspects of the requirement. Which governmental entity would be required to provide the notice? Would it be the police, when taking a crime report? The prosecutor prior to seeking an indictment or filing an information? Or perhaps the court at some other stage in the process? At what point would the right attach — when the crime is committed? When an arrest is made? . . .Does the term presume that the government entity providing notice must have assimilated the Supreme Court's latest jurisprudence interpreting victims' rights when giving notice? . . . . "Finally, Congress will be empowered . . . to enforce its provisions presumably including the question of how governmental entities must provide victims notice. Will this permit Congress to micromanage the policies and procedures of our state and local law enforcement agencies, prosecutors, and courts? I believe greater consideration must be given to these questions before a right to notice of the rights guaranteed by the amendment is included in the Constitution," S.Rept. 105-409 at 43-4 (additional views of Sen. Hatch).

[55] *E.g.*, S.J. Res. 1 (108th Cong.); H.J.Res. 48 (108th Cong.).

[56] Id.

[57] "(1) *Government*. Officers and employees of the Department of Justice and other departments and agencies of the United States engaged in the detection, investigation, or prosecution of crime shall make their best efforts to see that crime victims are notified of, and

accorded, the rights described in subsection (a). (2) *Advice of attorney*. The prosecutor shall advise the crime victim that the crime victim can seek the advice of an attorney with respect to the rights described in subsection (a). (3) *Notice*. Notice of release otherwise required pursuant to this chapter shall not be given if such notice may endanger the safety of any person," 18 U.S.C. 3771(c).

[58] *United States v. L.M.*, 425 F.Supp.2d 948, 957-58 (N.D. Iowa 2006)(denying victims the right to attend closed juvenile proceedings, but granting the government's request to notify them and to unseal the record of the proceedings except with respect to juvenile's identification and information that would lead to his identification).

[59] One witness, however, thought it more likely to confirm an intent to embrace civil proceedings, *Senate Hearing V* at 162; *House Hearing V* at 79 (statements of James Orenstein) ("Some public proceedings 'involving the crime' are civil in nature, and normally proceed without any participation by the executive branch of government. Here again, the change in language from S.J.Res. 3 [106th Cong.] could be problematic: that bill used the phrase 'relating to the crime' which the Senate Judiciary Committe noted would 'typically . . . be the criminal proceedings arising from the filed criminal charges, although other proceedings might also be related to the crime.' Senate Report at 30-31. A court interpreting the current bill might conclude that the change from 'relating to' to 'involving' was intended to make it easier to apply the Amendment to proceedings outside the criminal context "); see also, *Senate Hearing IV* at 122; *House Hearing IV* at 50.

[60] "Frequently, criminal defendants are suspected to have committed crimes for which they are never charged or for which charges are later dropped, even though significant evidence may exist that the defendant did indeed commit the crime. Do the victims of these crimes have rights under the proposed amendment? If so, are they the same as the rights of the victims of charged counts or of the defendant? Such victims, of course, would have the same rights to notice and allocution relating to conditional release, the acceptance of negotiated pleas (perhaps substantially complicating plea bargains) and sentencing," S.Rept. 105-409 at 42 (additional views of Sen. Hatch). Under existing federal law, sentencing courts are to consider "relevant conduct" that is "part of the same course of conduct or common scheme or plan as the offense of conviction," U.S.S.G. §1B1.3(a)(2), that includes misconduct for which the defendant has

never been charged or even for which he may have been acquitted, *United States v. Watts*, 519 U.S. 148 (1997).

[61] *But see*, S.Rept. 108-191 at 35 ("The release [which triggers a notification requirement] must be one 'relating to the crime.' This includes not only a release after a criminal conviction but also, for example, a release of a defendant found not guilty of a crime by reason of insanity and then hospitalized in custody for further treatment, or a release pursuant to a habitual sex offender statute ").

[62] 150 *Cong.Rec.* S4267-268 (daily ed. April 22, 2004)(remarks of Sens. Kyl and Feinstein)("Public proceedings include both trial level and appellate level court proceedings. . . I ask Senator Feinstein, if she can comment on her understanding of section (a)(2)? Mrs. FEINSTEIN. My understanding of this subsection is the same as the Senator's").

[63] *Compare*, S.Rept. 108-191 at 33-34, *with*, S.Rept. 106-254 at 30-1, S.Rept. 105-409 at 25-6.

[64] The right to notice of hearings at which an individual has a right to be heard is a component of due process under existing law. "The Supreme Court has long made clear that due process requires notice reasonably calculated to provide actual notice of the proceedings and a meaningful opportunity to be heard. In *City of West Covina v. Perkins*, [525 U.S. 234, 240] (1999), the Court explained the notice requirement in these words: A primary purpose of the notice required by the Due Process Clause is to ensure that the opportunity for a hearing is meaningful. See *Mullane v. Central Hanover Bank & Trust Co.*, 339 U.S. 306 (1950)('Th[e] right to be heard has little reality or worth unless one is informed that the matter [affecting one's property rights] is pending and can choose for himself whether to appear or default, acquiesce or contest')", *Nazarove v. INS*, 171 F.3d 478, 482-83 (7th Cir. 1999).

[65] S.Rept. 106-254 at 30 ("In rare mass victim cases (*i.e.*, those involving hundreds of victims), reasonable notice could be provided by mean[s] tailored to those unusual circumstances, such as notification by newspaper or television announcement"); *see also*, S.Rept. 105-409 at 25.

[66] *Small v. United States*, 136 F.3d 1334, 1336 (D.C.Cir. 1998)("'An elementary and fundamental requirement of due process in any proceeding which is to be accorded finality is notice reasonably calculated, under all the circumstances to apprise interested parties of the pendency of the action and afford them an opportunity to present their objections.' *Mullane v. Central Hanover Bank & Truest Co.*, 339

U.S. at 314. As *Mullane* made clear, the Due Process Clause does not demand actual, successful notice, but it does require a reasonable effort to give notice. '[P]rocess which is mere gesture is not due process. The means employed must be such as one desirous of actually informing the absentee might reasonably adopt to accomplish it.' *Mullane*, 339 U.S. at 315. . . . [T]he *Mullane* Court observed that '[c]hance alone brings to the attention of even a local resident an advertisement in small type inserted in the back pages of a newspaper.' *Id.* Almost fifty years after *Mullane*, in an increasingly populous and mobile nation, newspaper notices have virtually no chance of alerting an unwary person that he must act now forever lost his rights"). The Senate reports noted that "reasonableness" must be judged by the circumstances of an individual case. Thus, "[w]hile mailing a letter would be 'reasonable' notice of an upcoming parole release date, it would not be reasonable notice of the escape of a dangerous prisoner bent on taking revenge on his accuser," S.Rept. 108-191 at 35; S.Rept. 106-254 at 36;. S.Rept. 105-409 at 30.

[67] "For these rights to notice to be effective, notice must be sufficiently given in advance of a proceeding to give the crime victim the opportunity to arrange his or her affairs in order to be able to attend that proceeding and any scheduling of proceedings should take into account the victim's schedule to facilitate effective notice." 150 *Cong.Rec.* 4268 (daily ed. April 22, 2004)(remarks of Sen. Kyl).

[68] In the view of one commentator, "'Timely' notice would require that the victim be informed enough in advance of a public proceeding to be able reasonably to organize his or her affairs to attend," *Senate Hearing V* at 242 (statement of Steven T. Twist); see also, *Senate Hearing IV* at 183; *House Hearing IV* at 20 (statement of Steven T. Twist).

[69] *United States v. Turner*, 367 F.Supp.2d 319, 332 (E.D.N.Y. 2005)("Each of the three adjectives — 'reasonable, accurate, and timely' — is important: 'reasonable' provides vital flexibility; 'accurate' may well impose an affirmative obligation to advice victims of schedule changes (most states have similar statutory requirements); and 'timely' is designed to be a flexible concept that ensures a victim can reasonably arrange her affairs to attend the proceeding for which notice is given"); *see also United States v. Ingrassia*, 392 F.Supp.2d 493, 495 (E.D.N.Y. 2005)(describing an online victim notification system considered inadequate that provided outdated scheduling information).

[70] The section may apply to escapes and releases occurring after its effective date regardless of when the underlying crime occurred; many other jurisdictions apply the right with respect to self-identifying victims of prisoners sentenced after the effective date of the statutory provision creating or implementing the right, *e.g.*, N.Y.Crim.Pro.Law §380.50 (notice is provided by certified mail to victims who have submitted notification cards distributed to them shortly after the defendant is sentenced).

[71] Past proposals had a provision which declared, ". . . Nothing in this article shall provide grounds to . . . reopen any proceeding . . . except with respect to conditional release . . . ." *e.g.,* S.J.Res.3 (106th Cong.). Since the amendment has no similar prohibition on reopening at the petition of a victim, no bail exception is necessary. Of course, whether the initial bail hearing is delayed or the accused is re-arrested following the victim's petition to reopen, the result is the same — an accused is detained longer than would otherwise be the case in the name of victims' rights, S.Rept. 105-409 at 44 (additional views of Sen. Hatch)("This provision in particular has perhaps the greatest potential to collide with the legitimate right of defendants. All defendants and convicts have a constitutionally protected liberty interest in conditional release, once such release is granted. Permitting victims to move to reopen such proceedings or invalidate such rulings, would, of course, necessitate the re-arrest and detention of released defendants and convicts, likely implicating their liberty interest").

[72] *See United States v. Turner*, 367 F.Supp.2d 319, 324 (E.D.N.Y. 2005)("when it became apparent that the alleged victims here had not been given specific notice of the first two proceedings, I considered an adjournment as an alternative to further proceedings in violation of the victim's rights. Another alternative, and one that I concluded was preferable under the circumstances, was to order the government to provide a written summary or transcript of the proceedings to any victim who was denied notice and to make it clear that I would hear any victim with respect to whether the decision I made in the victim's absence should be reconsidered. I do not endorse this alternative as a routine substitute for conducting such proceedings without notice to victims — the statute plainly forbids such an approach. But where, as here, the result of the proceeding conduct in the victims' absence is one that does not appear to jeopardize any substantive (as opposed to procedural) right of the victim [since the defendant was detained rather than released on bail], the relief I ordered here seemed preferable to an

order that would require further incarceration of a criminal defendant without a substantive ruling on whether there exist conditions of release that satisfy the requirements of the Bail Reform Act").

[73] 18 U.S.C. 3771(c)(3)("Notice of release otherwise required pursuant to this chapter shall not be given if such notice may endanger the safety of any person").

[74] 150 *Cong.Rec.* S4269 (daily ed. April 22, 2004)("the notice section immediately following limits the right to notice of release where such notice may endanger the safety of the person being released. There are cases, particularly in domestic violence cases, where there is a danger posed by an intimate partner if the intimate partner is released. Such circumstances are not the norm, even in domestic violence cases as a category of cases. This exception should not be relied upon as an excuse to avoid notifying most victims")(remarks of Sen. Kyl).

[75] 150 *Cong. Rec.* S4269-270 (daily ed. April 22, 2004)("I want to turn to section 2, subsection (d)(2) because it is an unfortunate reality that in today's world there are crimes that result in multiple victims. The reality of those situations is that a court may find that the sheer number of victims is so large that it is impracticable to accord each victim the rights in this bill. The bill allows that when the court makes that finding on the record the court must then fashion a procedure that still gives effect to the bill and yet takes into account the impracticality. For instance, in the Oklahoma City bombing case the number of victims was tremendous and attendance at any one proceeding by all of them was impracticable so the court fashioned a procedure that allowed victims to attend the proceedings by closed circuit televison. This is merely one example. Another may be to allow victims with a right to speak to be heard in writing or through other methods. Importantly, courts must seek to identify methods that fit the case before that to ensure that despite numerosity of crime victims, the rights in this bill are given effect. Does the Senator agree with this reading of the bill? Mrs. FEINSTEIN. Absolutely.").

[76] The limitations of section 3771(d)(2) apply here as well ("In a case where the court finds that the number of crime victims makes it impracticable to accord all of the crime victims the rights described in subsection (a), the court shall fashion a reasonable procedure to give effect to this chapter that does not unduly complicate or prolong the proceedings").

[77] "*In all criminal prosecutions, the accused shall enjoy the right to a speedy and public trial, by an impartial jury* of the State and district

wherein the crime shall have been committed, which district shall have been previously ascertained by law, and to be informed of the nature and cause of the accusation; to be confronted with the witnesses against him; to have compulsory process for obtaining witnesses in his favor, and to have the Assistance of Counsel for his defence," U.S.Const. Amend. VI (emphasis added).

[78] *United States v. Gibbs*, 182 F.3d 408, 436 (6th Cir. 1999), citing, *United States v. Gagnon*, 470 U.S. 522, 526 (1985), and *Faretta v. California*, 422 U.S. 806, 819 n.15 (1975).

[79] *Woods v. Dugger*, 923 F.2d 1454, 1459-460 (11th Cir. 1991)(finding a Sixth Amendment violation in a case involving the murder of a prison guard, marked by extensive pretrial publicity, in a community where the prison system employed a substantial percentage of the population, and in which more than half of the members in attendance during the course of the trial were uniformed prison guards); *Norris v. Risley*, 918 F.2d 828, 834 (9th Cir.1990)(finding a Sixth Amendment violation in a kidnaping/rape case in which women wearing "Women Against Rape" buttons permeated the courtroom and its environs)("we find the risk unconstitutionally great that these large and boldly highlighted buttons tainted Norris's right to a fair trial both by eroding the presumption of innocence and by allowing extraneous, prejudicial considerations and cross-examination"). *Norris* also noted a similar view among the state courts, "A decision of the West Virginia Supreme Court is informative regarding the wearing of buttons during trial. State v. Franklin, 327 S.E.2d 449 (W.Va. 1985) involved a prosecution for driving under the influence of alcohol, resulting in death. During the trial, various spectators from an organization campaigning under the acronym MADD (Mothers Against Drunk Driving) wore buttons inscribed with the capital letters MADD. Most jurors knew what the initials stood for. In reversing the conviction and remanding for a new trial, the court noted that the trial court's 'cardinal failure . . . was to take no action whatever against a predominant group of ordinary citizens who were tooth and nail opposed to any finding that the defendant was not guilty.' Id. at 455," 918 F.2d at 832.

[80] VI WIGMORE ON EVIDENCE §§1837, 1838 (1940 ed.).

[81] F.R.Evid. 615("At the request of a party the court shall order witnesses excluded so that they cannot hear the testimony of other witnesses, and it may make the order of its own motion. This rule does not authorize exclusion of (1) a party who is a natural person, or

(2) an officer or employee of a party which is not a natural person designated as its representative by its attorney, (3) a person whose presence is shown by a party to be essential to the presentation of the party's cause, or (4) a person authorized by statute to be present").

[82] 18 U.S.C. 3510(b); 3593(c). *See also*, *United States v. McVeigh*, 958 F.Supp. 512, 514-15 (D.Colo. 1997)(permitting victims to attend trial with the observation that the court's control over any subsequent sentencing hearing would permit protective measures against any prejudicial impact). The *McVeigh* trial court had barred victim-witnesses from trial prior to the enactment of section 3510 and the amendment of section 3593(c). Following that initial sequestration order, the Court of Appeals had held that victim-witnesses had no standing based on 42 U.S.C. 10606 to seek mandamus in order to overturn the lower court's sequestration order, *United States v. McVeigh*, 106 F.3d 325, 334-35 (10th Cir. 1997).

[83] S.J.Res. 1 (108th Cong.); H.J.Res. 48 (108th Cong.); S.J.Res. 35 (107th Cong.); H.J.Res. 91 (107th Cong.); S.J.Res. 3 (106th Cong.); H.J.Res. 64 (106th Cong.). The exceptions were mentioned occurred early on, H.J.Res. 173 (104th Cong.)(the right "to be present at, every stage of the public proceedings, unless the court determines there is good cause for the victim not to be present"); H.J.Res. 174 (104th Cong.)("given the opportunity to be present at every proceeding in which those rights are extended to the accused or convicted offender"); S.J.Res. 52 (104th Cong.) (same).

[84] S.Rept. 108-191 at 35-6; S.Rept. 106-254 at 31, S.Rept. 105-409 at 26. *See also*, 150 *Cong.Rec.* 4268 (daily ed. April 22, 2004)(remarks of Sen. Feinstein)("This language was drafted in a way to ensure that the government would not be responsible for paying for the victim's travel and lodging to a place where they could attend the proceedings"); *United States v. Turner*, 367 F.Supp.2d 319, 332 (E.D.N.Y. 2005) ("This right effectively trumps Federal Rule of Evidence 615, and in doing so broadens a 1997 statute, 18 U.S.C. 3510, that was enacted in response to the trial court's exclusion of victims from the proceedings in the Oklahoma city bombing case on the ground that they might give victim impact testimony at a penalty phase. . . . [T]he right is phrased in the negative (*i.e.*, the crime victim has the right 'not to be excluded') rather than as an affirmative right to attend. This is to guard against arguments that the government has some affirmative duty to make it possible for indigent or incarcerated victims to be present in the courtroom. . . . The negative phrasing also

suggests that the fact that a properly notified victim cannot be present is not in itself a circumstance that requires a proceeding to be adjourned").

[85] S.Rept. 108-191 at 36; S.Rept. 106-254 at 31, S.Rept. 105-409 at 26.

[86] "The amendment works no change in the standards for closing hearings, but rather simply recognizes that nonpublic hearings take place," S.Rept. 108-191 at 34; S.Rept. 106-254 at 30; S.Rept. 105-409 at 25; *see also, United States v. L.M.*, 425 F.Supp. 948, 957 (N.D. Iowa 2006)(deciding to close juvenile proceedings and denying a motion for victim attendance).

[87] 18 U.S.C. 3771(b)("In any court proceeding involving an offense against a crime victim, the court shall ensure that the crime victim is afforded the rights described in subsection (a). Before making a determination described in subsection (a)(3), the court shall make every effort to permit the fullest attendance possible by the victim and shall consider reasonable alternatives to the exclusion of the victim from the criminal proceeding. The reasons for any decision denying relief under this chapter shall be clearly stated on the record.").

[88] *In re Mikhel*, 453 F.3d 1137, 1139 (9th Cir. 2006).

[89] The limitations of section 3771(d)(2) apply here as well ("In a case where the court finds that the number of crime victims makes it impracticable to accord all of the crime victims the rights described in subsection (a), the court shall fashion a reasonable procedure to give effect to this chapter that does not unduly complicate or prolong the proceedings").

[90] "A victim of violent crime shall have the right to . . . reasonably to be heard at public release, plea, sentencing, reprieve, and pardon proceedings," S.J.Res. 1 (108th Cong.); H.J.Res. 48 (108th Cong.).

[91] S.Rept. 105- 409, at 27, 28 (1998)("Victims have no right to 'veto' any release decision by the court, simply to provide relevant information that the court can consider in making its determination about release. . . . Once again, the victim is given no right of veto over any plea. No doubt some victims may wish to see nothing less than the maximum possible penalty (or minimum possible) for a defendant. Under the amendment, the court will receive this information, along with that provided by prosecutions and defendants, and give it the weight it believes is appropriate deciding whether to accept a plea"); S.Rept. 106-254, at 32, 33 (2000); S.Rept. 108-191, at 36, 37 (2003).

[92] *Bell v. Wolfish,* 441 U.S. 520, 535 n.16 (1979)("Due process requires that a pretrial detainee not be punished"); *North Carolina v. Pearce*,

395 U.S. 711, 725 (1969)("Due process of law, then, requires that vindictiveness against a defendant [based on the exercise of a constitutional right] must play no part in the sentence he receives after trial").

[93] H.J.Res. 64 (106th Cong.)(" . . . a victim of a crime . . . shall have the right . . . to be heard, if present, and to submit a statement at all such proceedings to determine a conditional release from custody, an acceptance of a negotiated plea, or a sentence. . . "); S.J.Res. 3 (106th Cong.).

[94] S.Rept. 108-191, at 38 (2003)("The victim's right is to be 'heard.' The right to make an oral statement is conditioned on the victim's presence in the courtroom. As discussed above, it does not confer on victims a right to have the government transport them to the relevant proceeding").

[95] *United States v. Degenhardt*, 405 F.Supp.2d 1341, (D. Utah 2005)("the CVRA gives crime victims the right to be 'reasonably heard' at sentencing. One possible interpretation of this phrase is that victims have a right to be heard via a *written* submission to the court, such as a victim impact form. . . Such a construction, however, would defy the intentions of the CVRA's drafters, ignoring the fact that defendants and prosecutors make oral statements at sentencing, and disregard the rationales underlying victim allocution. For all these reasons the court concludes that the CVRA gives victims the right to speak directly the judge at sentencing"); *Kenna v. District Court*, 435 F.3d 1011, 1016 (9th Cir. 2006)("The statements of the sponsors of the CVRA and the committee report for the proposed constitutional amendment disclose a clear congressional intent to give crime victims the right to speak at proceedings covered by the CVRA").

[96] *United States v. Marcello*, 370 F.Supp.2d745, (N.D. Ill. 2005)("In light of the statute's clear language, the purpose of the detention hearing and the content of the testimony sought to be introduced in this case, I find that this victim's right to be reasonably heard could be satisfied through means other than an oral statement").

[97] *Kenna v. District Court*, 435 F.3d at 1018 (Friedman, J., dubitante)("My concern is that the court seems to hold that a victim has an absolute right to speak at sentencing no matter what the circumstances. . . . [I]t is not clear to me that this statute goes that far. I would leave that issue open and issue an opinion of more limited scope").

[98] S.Rept. 105-409, at 29 (1998)("a court may set reasonable limits on the length and content of statements"); S.Rept. 106-254, at 34 (same); note, however, that reference to content was omitted without explanation in the final report, S.Rept. 108-191, at 38 ("a court may set reasonable limits on the length of statements, but should not require the victim to submit a statement for approval before it is offered").

[99] *House Hearings V*, at 41 (statement of Steven J. Twist); *Senate Hearings V*, at 253.

[100] 150 *Cong.Rec.* S4268 (daily ed. April 22, 2004)(remarks of Sen.Kyl).

[101] H.J.Res. 173 (104th Cong.) ("to comment at any such proceeding involving the possible release of the defendant from custody"); S.J.Res. 52 (104th Cong.)("to be heard at any proceeding involving . . . a release from custody").

[102] S.J.Res. 3 (106th Cong.)("A victim of a crime . . . shall have the right. . . to be heard, if present, and to submit a statement at all such proceedings to determine a condition release from custody. . . to the foregoing rights at as parole proceeding that is not public, to the extent those rights are afforded to the convicted offender"); H.J.Res. 64 (106th Cong.).

[103] S.J.Res.1 (108th Cong.) ("A victim shall have the right . . . to be heard at public release . . . reprieve, and pardon proceedings . . ."); H.J.Res. 48 (108th Cong.).

[104] *Cf., Senate Hearing V; House Hearing V* at 35 (statement of Steven T. Twist)("The right would also extend to post-conviction public release proceedings, for example parole or conditional release hearings. Jurisdictions that have abolished parole in favor of truth in sentencing regimes may still have conditional release. Only if the jurisdiction also has a 'public proceeding' prior to such a conditional release would the right attach"); see also, *Senate Hearing IV* at 186-87; *House Hearing IV* at 22 (statement of Steven T. Twist).

[105] S.Rept. 108-191, at 38 (2003)("The victim's right to be heard does not extend to the guilt determination phase of trials, although victims may, of course, be called as a witness by either party. The Committee, however, intends no modification of the current law, with deep historical roots, allowing a crime victim's attorney to participate in the prosecution").

[106] Cassell, *Recognizing Victims in the Federal Rules of Criminal Procedure: Proposed Amendments in Light of the Crime Victims'*

Rights Act, 2005 BRIGHAM YOUNG UNIVERSITY LAW REVIEW 835, 918.

[107] *Cf.,* 150 *Cong.Rec.* S4268 (daily ed. April 22, 2004)(remarks of Sens. Kyl and Feinstein) (noting that the right to attend public court proceedings was not intended to convey a right to attend closed proceedings such those before the grand jury or those closed out of concern for national security); *United States v. L.M.*, 425 F.Supp. 948, 957 (N.D. Iowa 2006) (deciding to close juvenile proceedings and denying motion for victim attendance).

[108] Of course, even if the right to be heard applies only to public proceedings in the district court, a later subsection of section 3771 allows victims to enforce their rights through a writ of mandamus at the appellate level, 18 U.S.C. 3771(d)(3).

[109] *United States v. Turner*, 367 F.Supp.2d 319, 336 (E.D.N.Y. 2005)("A defendant's initial appearance pursuant to F.R.Crim.P. 5 is a public proceeding and presumptively includes consideration of whether the accused offender will be released. See 18 U.S.C. 3142(a),(f). Accordingly, victims must be given reasonable, accurate, and timely notice of the proceeding, as well as an opportunity to be heard with respect to bail. Of course, such application of the notice requirement to the initial appearance raises an obvious practical difficulty, in that the defendant is generally required to be brought before the magistrate judge 'without unnecessary delay.' F.R.Crim.P. 5(a)(1). The question is whether it is either 'necessary' within the meaning of Rule 5 or "reasonable' within the meaning of §3771(a)(2) to delay the initial appearance to ensure timely notice to a victim. Answering that question may well require a case-by-case inquiry into the circumstances that might indicate that an absent victim is uniquely able to address the issue of the defendant's release. I had no such indication in this case, and believe that the procedure I followed — proceeding promptly with the initial appearance and (belatedly) requiring the government to notify victims of the result and of their right to request reconsideration of relevant decisions made in their absence — reasonably balances the competing interests at stake").

[110] Administrative Office of the United States Courts, *Judicial Business of the United States Courts*, 258 (2005)(only 3,315 of the 77,339 defendants convicted of federal crimes in the fiscal year ending in September 30, 2005, were found guilty by a judge or jury following a criminal trial; the rest pled guilty or nolo contendere).

[111] In addition to extraordinarily broad discretion to initiate or abandon a prosecution, *Wayte v. United States*, 470 U.S. 598 (1985); *Town of Newton v. Rumery*, 480 U.S. 386 (1987), prosecutors play an important role in sentencing, *e.g.*, 18 U.S.C. 3553(b)(federal court may depart from the federal sentencing guidelines upon the motion of the prosecutor); 18 U.S.C. 3553(e)(federal court may sentence a defendant below an otherwise mandatory minimum term of imprisonment upon the motion of the prosecutor).

[112] *E.g.*, *Miles v. Dorsey*, 61 F.3d 1459 (10th Cir. 1995); *United States v. Pollard*, 959 F.2d 1011 (D.C.Cir. 1992).

[113] *Cf.*, *Libretti v. United States*, 516 U.S. 29 (1995)(government agreed to limit charges and make a favorable sentencing recommendation in exchange for the defendant's guilty plea and his agreement to transfer all property that would have been subject to criminal forfeiture upon his conviction).

[114] *E.g.*, 18 U.S.C. 6001-6005 (witness immunity).

[115] *E.g.*, 18 U.S.C. 3521 (witness relocation and protection).

[116] *E.g.*, 18 U.S.C. 3059 (rewards); 18 U.S.C. 3059A (rewards for crimes against financial institutions); 18 U.S.C. 3071-3077 (rewards for information relating to terrorism).

[117] "The victim has two interests in the plea bargain decision. One interest is financial: the victim is interested in restitution being imposed as part of the sentence. Thus in a charge bargain, the victim wants to insure that the defendant pleads to a charge sufficiently serious to allow restitution; and in a sentence bargain, the victim wants to advocate an award of restitution. The victim's second interest is retribution, or revenge: the victim feels he or she has been violated and that the criminal's punishment should be severe. Therefore, in a charge bargain, the victim would want the defendant to plead guilty to a serious charge, and in a sentence bargain, the victim would want a significant sentence imposed," Walling, *Victim Participation in Plea Bargains*, 65 WASHINGTON UNIVERSITY LAW QUARTERLY 301, 307-8 (1987).

[118] *E.g.*, *The Proper Standard for Self-Defense in New York: Should* People v. Goetz *Be Viewed as Judicial Legislation or Judicial Restraint*, 39 SYRACUSE LAW REVIEW 874 (1988)(discussing prosecution of a subway rider who shot the four young men he claimed attempted to rob him; the subway rider was subsequently prosecuted and convicted for unlawful possession of a handgun).

[119] The Senate committee reports, on the question of when public hearings might be closed thus removing the trigger for the rights under earlier proposals, opined that, "while plea proceedings are generally open to the public, a court might decide to close a proceeding in which an organized crime underling would plead guilty and agree to testify against his bosses," S.Rept. 108-191 at 34; S.Rept. 106-254 at 30; S.Rept. 105-409 at 25.

[120] *Cf., In re W.R. Huff Asset Management Co., LLC*, 409 F.3d 555, 564 (2d Cir. 2005) ("Nothing in CVRA requires the Government to seek approval from crime victims before negotiating or entering into a settlement agreement").

[121] S.Rept. 108-191 at 36 ("Victims have no right to 'veto' any release decision by a court, rather simply to provide relevant information that the court can consider in making its determination about release"); see also, *Senate Hearing IV* at187; *House Hearing IV* at 22-3 (statement of Steven J. Twist), quoting S.Rept. 106-254 at 33("the victim is given no right of veto over any plea. No doubt, some victims may wish to see nothing less than the maximum possible penalty (or minimum possible penalty) for a defendant. Under the amendment, the court will receive this information, along with that provided by prosecutors and defendants, and give it the weight it believes is appropriate deciding whether to accept a plea").

[122] In *Booth v. Maryland*, 482 U.S. 496 (1987), the Supreme Court held that the Eighth Amendment did not permit the presentation of victim impact evidence to a sentencing jury in a death penalty case; in *Payne v. Tennessee*, 501 U.S. 808 (1991), it repudiated *Booth* and declared that victim impact statements were not inherently suspect.

[123] *Welch v. Sirmons*, 451 F.3d 675, 703 (10th Cir. 2006); *see also*, *United States v. Brown*, 441 F.3d 1330, 1351 (11th Cir. 2006); *Humphries v. Ozmint*, 397 F.3d 206, 217 (4th Cir. 2005); *United States v. Bernard*, 299 F.3d 467, 480 (5th Cir. 2002); *Parker v. Bowersox*, 188 F.3d 9233, 931 (8th Cir. 1999).

[124] *United States v. Degenhardt*, 405 F.Supp.2d 1341, 1345 (D. Utah 2005)("the CVRA gives crime victims the right to be 'reasonably heard' at sentencing. One possible interpretation of this phrase is that victims have a right to be heard via a *written* submission to the court, such as a victim impact form. . . Such a construction, however, would defy the intentions of the CVRA's drafters, ignoring the fact that defendants and prosecutors make oral statements at sentencing, and disregard the rationales underlying victim allocution. For all these

reasons the court concludes that the CVRA gives victims the right to speak directly the judge at sentencing"); *Kenna v. District Court*, 435 F.3d 1011, 1016 (9th Cir. 2006)("The statements of the sponsors of the CVRA and the committee report for the proposed constitutional amendment disclose a clear congressional intent to give crime victims the right to speak at proceedings covered by the CVRA"); *but see*, 435 F.3d at 1018 (Friedman, J., dubitante)("My concern is that the court seems to hold that a victim has an absolute right to speak at sentencing no matter what the circumstances. . . . [I]t is not clear to me that this statute goes that far. I would leave that issue open and issue an opinion of more limited scope").

[125] Congress abolished parole for those convicted of federal crimes committed after November 1, 1987, P.L. 98-473, 98 Stat. 2027 (1984). Parole is included in the sentencing regime relating to crimes committed in the District, D.C.CODE §§24-401 to 24-468.

[126] U.S.Const. Art.II, §2, cl.1.

[127] 28 C.F.R. §§0.35, 0.36.

[128] "In any appeal in a criminal case, the Government *may* assert as error the district court's denial of any crime victim's right in the proceeding to which the appeal relates. . . Nothing in this chapter shall be construed to impair the prosecutorial discretion of the Attorney General or any officer under his direction," 18 U.S.C. 3771(d)(4), (6)(emphasis added).

[129] *In re W.R. Huff Asset Management Co., LLC*, 409 F.3d 555, 564 (2d Cir. 2005)("no petitioner has alleged that it asked the Government to confer with it and was denied the opportunity to do so").

[130] S.J.Res. 1 (108th Cong.), H.J.Res. 48 (108th Cong.), S.J.Res. 35 (107th Cong.), H.J.Res. 91 (107th Cong.).

[131] S.J.Res. 65 (104th Cong.); H.J.Res. 173 (104th Cong.)(the right "to have the court order restitution from the defendant upon conviction").

[132] H.J.Res. 174 (104th Cong.); S.J.Res. 52 (104th Cong.).

[133] H.J.Res. 71 (105th Cong.)(the right "to an order of restitution from the convicted offender"); H.J.Res. 129 (105th Cong.)(same); S.J.Res.6 (105th Cong.)(same); S.J.Res.44 (105th Cong.)(same); H.J.Res. 64 (106th Cong.)(same); S.J.Res.3 (106th Cong.)(same).

[134] This construction might have drawn some support from the observation in the Senate report that with respect to this language in an earlier proposal, "[t]he right is, of course, limited to 'convicted' defendants, that is, those who pled guilty, are found guilty, or enter a plea of no contest," S.Rept. 105-409 at 32. Unless they are prosecuted

as adults, juveniles do not plead guilty, are not found guilty, nor do they enter nolo pleas. They confess to being or are found delinquent, or in need of supervision, or neglected, but they are not convicted. The Committee also declared that it had "previously explained [its] philosophy in some detail in connection with the Mandatory Victim Restitution Act, codified at 18 U.S.C. §§3663A and 3664, and *intends that this right operate in a similar fashion*," S.Rept. 105-409 at 31 (emphasis added). Even though the Mandatory Victim Restitution Act applies to juveniles tried and convicted as adults, it does *not* apply to findings of delinquency or other dispositions following juvenile proceedings.

[135] *Wheat v. United States*, 486 U.S. 153, 159 (1988); *United States v. Monsanto*, 491 U.S. 600, 616 (1989)("if the Government may, post-trial, forbid the use of forfeited assets to pay an attorney, then surely no constitutional violation occurs when, after probable cause is adequately established, the Government obtains an order barring a defendant from frustrating that end by dissipating his assets prior to trial").

[136] *Compare, United States v. Martinez*, 978 F.Supp. 1442 (D.N.Mex. 1997)(refusing to issue mandatory restitution order for the benefit of illegal Indian casino which had been the victim of an armed robbery), *with, United States v. Bonetti*, 277 F.3d 441 (4th Cir. 2002) (holding that an illegal immigrant was entitled to restitution from those who harbored her under abusive conditions).

[137] 150 *Cong. Rec.* S4268 (daily ed. April 22, 2004)(remarks of Sen. Kyl)("I would like to turn now to the section on restitution, section 2, (a)(6). This section provides the right to full and timely restitution as provided in law. This right, together with the other rights in the act to be heard and confer with the Government's attorney in this act, means that existing restitution laws will be more effective").

[138] *In re W.R.Huff Asset Management Co., LLC*, 409 F.3d 555, 563 (2d Cir. 2005).

[139] "In all criminal prosecutions, the accused shall enjoy the right to a speedy and public trial. . . ." U.S.Const. Amend. VI.

[140] *Klopfer v. North Carolina*, 386 U.S. 213 (1967).

[141] *E.g.*, R.I.CONST. art.1, §10; S.C.CONST. art.I, §14.

[142] *E.g.*, *State:* CONN.SUPER.CT.R. §§956B to 956F; DEL.SUPER.CT.CRIM.R. 48 (b); FLA.R. CRIM.P. 3.191; GA.CODE ANN. §§17-7-170 to 17-7-171. *Federal:* 18 U.S.C. 3161-3174.

[143] Cassell, *Balancing the Scales of Justice: The Case for and the Effects of Utah's Victims' Rights Amendment*, 1994 UTAH LAW REVIEW 1373, 140.

[144] *E.g.*, Kelly, *Victims' Perceptions of Criminal Justice*, 11 PEPPERDINE LAW REVIEW 15, 19-20 (1984); *contra*, Henderson, *The Wrongs of Victim's Rights*, 37 STANFORD LAW REVIEW 937, 974-77 (1985).

[145] *E.g.* LA.REV.STAT.ANN. §46:1844 [J.] ("The victim shall have the right to a speedy disposition and prompt and final conclusion of the case after conviction and sentencing"); N.H.REV.STAT.ANN. §21-M:8-k.

[146] 42 U.S.C. 10606 nt. ("It is the sense of Congress that the States should make every effort to adopt the following goals of the Victims of Crime Bill of Rights: . . . (4) Victims of crime should have the right to a reasonable assurance that the accused will be tried in an expeditious manner").

[147] H.J.Res. 174 (104th Cong.) ("the victim shall have the following rights: . . . to a speedy trial, a final conclusion free from unreasonable delay. . ."); S.J.Res. 52 (104th Cong.)(same); S.Rept. 108-191 at 40 (2003)("Just as defendants currently have a right to a 'speedy trial,' this provision will give victims a protected right to have their interests to a reasonably prompt conclusion of a trial considered . . . In determining what delay is 'unreasonable,' the courts can look to the precedents that exist interpreting a defendant's right to a speedy trial"); see also, S.Rept. 105-409 at 19 (1998); S.Rept. 106-254 at 23 (2000).

[148] " H.J.Res. 174 (104th Cong.); S.J.Res. 52 (104th Cong.).

[149] H.J.Res. 173 (104th Cong.) ("any victim shall have the right . . . to have the proceedings resolved in a prompt and timely manner"); S.J.Res. 65 (104th Cong.)("Victims . . . shall have the rights . . . to a final disposition free form unreasonable delay").

[150] S.J.Res. 44 (105th Cong.)("Each victim . . . shall have the rights. . .to consideration for the interest of the victim in *a trial* free from unreasonable delay"); H.J.Res. 129 (105th Cong.)(same); S.J.Res. 6 (105th Cong.) ("Each victim . . . shall have the rights . . .to a *final disposition of the proceedings* relating to the crime free from unreasonable delay"); H.J.Res. 71 (105th Cong.) (" . . . a victim . . . shall have the right . . . to seek relief from an unreasonable delay of the *final disposition of the proceedings* relating to the crime") (emphasis added in each instance).

[151] H.J.Res. 64 (106th Cong); S.J.Res. 3(106th Cong.).

[152] S.J.Res. 1 (108th Cong.); H.J.Res. 48 (108th Cong.)

[153] S.Rept. 108-191 at 19 (2003).

[154] *United States v. McDaniel*, 411 F.Supp.2d 1323, 1325 (D.Utah 2005)(refusing to allow last minute substitution of defense counsel based in part upon the victim's right to proceedings free from unreasonable delay).

[155] *In re W.R.Huff Asset Management Co., LLC*, 409 F.3d 555, 559-60 (2d Cir. 2005)(refusing to find abuse of discretion in the trial court's refusal to approve more extensive but time consuming procedures to identify additional victims of a large scale fraud).

[156] *E.g.*, ALASKA CONST. Art.I, §24 (right to be treated with dignity, respect and fairness); ARIZ.CONST. Art.2, §2.1 (same); COLO.REV.STAT.ANN. §24-4.1-302.5 (fairness, respect and dignity); HAW.REV.STAT. §801D-1 (dignity, respect, courtesy and sensitivity); IDAHO CONST. Art.1, §22 and IDAHO CODE §19-5306 (right to be treated with fairness, respect, dignity and privacy); ILL.CONST. Art.1, §8.1 (right to be treated with fairness and respect for their dignity and privacy), ILL.COMP.LAWS ANN. ch.725 §120/2 (same); KAN.STAT.ANN. §74-7333 (fair[ness], compassion, respect for dignity and privacy and suffer a minimum of unnecessary inconvenience); LA.CONST. art.1, §25 (fairness, dignity, and respect); MD. CONST. art. 47 (dignity, respect and sensitivity); MICH.CONST. Art.1, §24 (fairness and respect for dignity and privacy); MONT. CODE ANN. §46-24-101 (fair and proper treatment); N.H.REV.STAT.ANN. §21-M:8-k (right to be treated with fairness and respect for their dignity and privacy throughout the criminal justice process); N.J.CONST. Art.1, ¶22 (fairness, compassion and respect), N.J.STAT.ANN. §52:4B-36 (dignity and compassion); N.MEX.CONST. Art.II, §24 (fairness and respect for dignity and privacy), N.M.STAT. ANN. §31-26-2 (dignity, respect and sensitivity); OHIO CONST. Art.I, §10a (fairness, dignity and respect); OKLA.CONST. Art.2, §34 (same); ORE.CONST. Art.I, §42 (due dignity and respect); PA.STAT.ANN. tit.18 §11.102 (dignity, respect, courtesy and sensitivity); R.I.CONST. Art. 23 (dignity, respect and sensitivity); TENN.CODE ANN. §40-38-102 (dignity and compassion); TEX.CONST. Art.1, §30 (fairness and respect for dignity and privacy); UTAH CONST. Art.1, §28 (fairness, respect, and dignity); VT.STAT. ANN. tit.13 §5303 (courtesy and sensitivity); VA.CODE ANN. §19.2-11.01 (dignity, respect and sensitivity); WASH.CONST. Art.1, §35

(dignity and respect); WIS.CONST. Art.I, §9m (fairness, dignity and respect for privacy); WYO.STAT. §1-40-203 (compassion, respect and sensitivity).

[157] *United States v. Turner*, 367 F.Supp.2d 319, 323 (E.D.N.Y. 2005)("While some proactive steps seem to be required, the statute just as clearly does not, in most circumstances, require courts to adopt every conceivable procedure that might protect the exercise of victims' rights. Specifically, it is only with respect to orders denying a victim's right to attend court proceedings that judges are directed to 'make every effort' to find reasonable alternatives to exclusion. 18 U.S.C. 3771(b). There is a lot of ground between extending some effort to 'ensure' that victims are afforded their rights and making 'every effort' to do so.").

[158] *Cf., In re W.R.Huff Asset Management Co., LLC*, 409 F.3d 555, 562 (2d Cir. 2005) ("Similarly, the CVRA [18 U.S.C. 3771] provides that the determination to 'ensure' that the crime victim is afforded the rights enumerated in the CVRA is entrusted to the district court to make").

[159] 150 *Cong.Rec.* S4269 (daily ed. April 22, 2004)(remarks of Sen. Kyl)("where there is a material conflict between the government's attorney and the crime victim, this provision protects the crime victims' rights. This means that if the government lawyers interpret a right differently from a victim, urge a very narrow interpretation of a right, or do not believe a right should be asserted, they are in conflict with the victim and this provision requires that they inform the victim of this and direct the victim to independent counsel, such as the legal clinics for crime victims contemplated under this law. This is an important protection for crime victims because it ensures the independent and individual nature of their rights").

[160] 150 *Cong.Rec.* S4269 (daily ed. April 22, 2004)(remarks of Sen. Feinstein)("this [provision allows a crime victim to enter the criminal trial court during proceedings involving the crime against the victim and assert the rights provided by this bill. This provision ensures that crime victims have standing to be heard in trial courts so that they are heard at the very moment when their rights are at stake and this, in turn, forces the criminal justice system to be responsive to a victim's rights in a timely way. Importantly, however, the bill does not allow the defendant in the case to assert any of the victim's rights to obtain relief. . . . The provision allows the crime victim's representative and the attorney for the government to go into a criminal trial court and

assert the crime victim's rights. The inclusions of representative and the government's attorney in the provision are important for a number of reasons. First, allowing a representative to assert a crime victim's rights ensures that where a crime victim is unable to assert the rights on his or her own for any reason, including incapacity, incompetence, minority, or death, those rights are not lost. . . . Second, a crime victim may choose to enlist a private attorney to represent him or her in the criminal case — this provision allows that attorney to enter an appearance on behalf of the victim in the criminal trial court and assert the victim's rights. The provision also recognizes that, at times, the government's attorney may be best situated to assert a crime victim's rights either because the crime victim is not available at a particular point in the trial or because, at times, the crime victim's interests coincide with those of the government and it makes sense for a single person to express those joint interests. Importantly, however, the provision does not mean that the government's attorney has the authority to compromise or co-opt a victim's right. The rights provided in this bill are personal to the individual crime victim and it is that crime victim that has the final word regarding which of the specific rights to assert and when. Waiver of any of the individual rights provided can only happen by the victim's affirmative waiver of that specific right").

[161] *In re Mikhel*, 543 F.3d 1137, 1138 (9th Cir. 2006)(mandamus petition following partial trial exclusion of victim-witnesses)("Although the United States is clearly not the 'victim' in this case, it is proper that the government bring this petition because §3771 provides that 'the attorney for the government may assert the rights described in subsection (a)'"); *United States v. L.M.*, 425 F.Supp.2d 948 (N.D.Iowa 2006)(exclusion of the deceased family members from closed juvenile transfer hearing)("The parties also agree that the government has standing to assert the CVRA rights of T.L.'s family members").

[162] *In re Mikhel*, 453 F.3d 1137, 1138 n.1(9th Cir. 2006); 150 *Cong.Rec.* H8188 (Oct. 6, 2004)(remarks of Rep. Sensenbrenner)("The government and or the crime victim can then seek a writ of mandamus from the appropriate Court of Appeals to ensure that the crime victim's rights are protected").

[163] S.J.Res. 3 (106th Cong.)("Nothing in this article shall provide grounds to stay or continue any trial. . ."); H.J.Res. 71 (105th Cong.)(". . . nothing in this article shall provide grounds for the victim to . . . obtain a stay of trial. . .").

[164] S.J.Res. 1 (108th Cong.); H.J.Res. 48 (108th Cong.).

[165] "The provision provides that [the] court shall take the writ and shall order the relief necessary to protect the crime victim's right. This provision is critical for a couple of reasons. First, it gives the victim standing to appear before the appellate courts of this country and ask for review of a possible error below. Second, while mandamus is discretionary, this provision means that courts must review these cases. Appellate review of denials of victims' right is just as important as the initial assertion of a victim's right. This provision ensures review and encourages courts to broadly defend the victims' rights. "Mr. President, does Senator Kyl agree? "Mr. KLY. Absolutely. Without the right to seek appellate review and a guarantee that the appellate court will hear the appeal and order relief, a victim is left to the mercy of the very trial court that may have erred. This country's appellate courts are designed to remedy errors of lower courts and this provision requires them to do so for victim's rights. For a victims right to truly be honored, a victim must be able to assert the rights in trial courts, to then be able to have denials of those rights reviewed at the appellate level, and to have the appellate court take the appeal and order relief. By providing for all of this, this bill ensures that victims' rights will have meaning." 150 *Cong.Rec.* S4270 (daily ed. April 22, 2004) (remarks of Sens. Feinstein and Kyl).

[166] *Cheney v. United States District Court*, 542 U.S. 367, 380 (2004).

[167] *In re W.R.Huff Asset Management Co., LLC,* 409 F.3d 555, 562 (2d Cir. 2005).

[168] *Id.*

[169] *Id.* at 562-63, citing, *Pierce v. Underwood*, 487 U.S. 552 (1988).

[170] *Kenna v. United States District Court*, 435 F.3d 1011, 1017 (9th. Cir. 2006).

[171] S.J.Res. 65 (104th Cong.)(". . . nothing in this article shall provide grounds for the victim to challenge a charging decision or a conviction, obtain a stay of trail, or compel a new trial"); H.J.Res. 71 (105th Cong.).

[172] H.J.Res. 64 (106th Cong.)("Nothing in this article shall provide grounds to stay or continue any trial, reopen any proceeding or invalidate any ruling, except with respect to conditional release or restitution or to provide rights guaranteed by this article in future proceedings, without staying or continuing a trial").

[173] H.J.Res. 91 (107th Cong.); S.J.Res. 1 (108th Cong.).

[174] *E.g.*, S.J.Res. 44 (105th Cong.); H.J.Res. 179 (105th Cong.).

[175] *E.g.*, S.J.Res. 65 (104th Cong.)("nor shall anything in this article provide grounds for the accused or convicted offender to obtain any form of relief"); S.J. Res. 6 (105th Cong.); H.J.Res. 88 (107th Cong.); S.J.Res. 1 (108th Cong.).

[176] "Importantly, however, the bill does not allow the defendant in the case to assert any of the victim's rights to obtain relief. This prohibition prevents the individual accused of the crime from distorting a right intended for the benefit of the individual victim into a weapon against justice," 150 *Cong.Rec.* S4269 (April 22, 2004)(remarks of Sen. Feinstein).

[177] *E.g.*, H.J.Res. 10 (108th Cong.); S.J.Res. 65 (104th Cong.).

[178] *See also*, "This provision demonstrates that victim's rights are not intended to be, nor are they, an attack on defendants' protections against double jeopardy," 150 *Cong.Rec.* S4270 (April 22, 2004)(remarks of Sen. Feinstein).

[179] S.Rept. 108-191, at 34 (2003)("In rare mass victim cases (i.e., those involving hundreds of victims), reasonable notice could be provided to means tailored to those unusual circumstances, such as notification by newspaper or television announcement"); S.Rept. 106-254, at 30 (2000).

[180] S.J.Res. 1 (108th Cong.)("These rights shall not be restricted except when and to the degree dictated by a substantial interest in public safety or the administration of criminal justice, or by compelling necessity"); S.Rept. 108-191, at 41 (2003)("The amendment does not impose a straightjacket that would prevent the proper handing of unusual situations. The restrictions language in the amendment explicitly recognizes that in certain rare circumstances restrictions may need to be created to victims' rights. . . For instance, for a crime perpetrated against hundreds of victims, it may be impractical or even impossible to give all victims the right to be physically present in the courtroom. . . Similar restrictions on the number of persons allowed to present oral statements might be appropriate in rare cases involving large numbers of victims").

[181] 150 *Cong.Rec.* S 4269-270 (April 22, 2004)(remarks of Sen. Kyl and Sen. Feinstein).

[182] *E.g.*, S.J.Res.1 (108th Cong.)("Nothing in this article shall be construed to . . . authorize any claim for damages"); S.J.Res. 65 (104th Cong.)(". . . nor shall anything in this article give rise to a claim for damages against the United States, a State, a political subdivision, or a public official").

[183] S.Rept. 108-191 at 42 (2003) ("The limiting language in the provision also prevents the possibility that the amendment might be construed by courts as requiring the appointment of counsel at state expense to assist victims. Cf. *Gideon v. Wainwright*, 372 U.S. 335 (1963)(requiring counsel for indigent criminal defendants)"); S.Rept. 105-409 at 35 (1998); S.Rept. 106-254 at 41(2000).

[184] 150 *Cong.Rec.* S4267 (daily ed. April 22, 2004)(remarks of Sen. Kyl)("The act before us, in addition to setting forth the rights and providing a remedy for the victims of crime, has an authorization of funding. Let me describe that authorization. . . $7 million to the Office of Victims of Crime for the National Crime Victim Law Institute to provide grants and assistance to lawyers to help victims of crime in court. It is the only entity in the country that provides lawyers for victims in criminal cases. . .").

[185] 150 *Cong.Rec.* S4272 (daily ed. April 22, 2004)(remarks of Sen. Leahy).

[186] United States Department of Justice, Office of Justice Programs, Office of Victims of Crime, *Attorney General Guidelines for Victim and Witness Assistance* (May 2005), available on September 27, 2006 at, [http://www.usdoj.gov/olp/final.pdf].

INDEX

A

B

C

D

E

F

G

H

I

R

S

T

U

V

W

Y